THEMATIC UN...

Things That Go

Written by Cynthia Holzschuher

Edited by Charlene Stout

Illustrated by Ken Tunell

Teacher Created Materials, Inc.
P.O. Box 1040
Huntington Beach, CA 92647
©1996 Teacher Created Materials, Inc.
Made in U.S.A.

ISBN 1-57690-111-4

Table of Contents

Introduction

Things That Go contains three lively whole language thematic units that are created specifically for use with children at the early childhood level. Each of the mini-units and core literature selections—*Cars and Trucks and Things That Go, First Flight,* and *Big City Port*—is the basis for many related creative activities that extend across the curriculum, addressing all learning modalities. These all-time favorite books set the stage for reading, establishing a "Reading is fun!" atmosphere and extending the concepts encountered. Directions for student-made books, singing games, snacks, crafts, and an exciting culminating activity allow the students to synthesize their knowledge and create products which can be shared beyond the classroom.

This thematic unit includes:

- **literature selections**—summaries of the three children's books with suggestions for related lessons and reproducible activity pages that cross the curriculum

- **poetry**—original poetry with suggestions for enabling students to write and publish their own poems

- **language experience and writing ideas**—suggestions for lessons and activities, as well as many student-made books, big and little, related to the literature selections

- **bulletin board ideas**—ideas and plans for interactive boards

- **curriculum connections**—relates the unit to language arts, math, science/social studies, art, music and life skills

- **group projects**—encourage cooperative learning and sharing in both small groups and whole class activities.

- **culminating activity**—synthesizes their learning with an appealing shared activity

- **bibliography**—lists literature, nonfiction books, audio visual aids, and computer software related to the transportation theme

---

To keep this valuable resource intact so it can be used year after year, you may wish to punch three holes in the pages and store them in a three-ring binder.

Introduction *(cont.)*

Why Balance Basic Skills and Whole Language?

The strength of a whole language approach is that it involves children in using all modes of communication—reading, writing, listening, illustrating, and interacting. Communication skills are interconnected and integrated into lessons that emphasize the whole of language. Balancing this approach is our knowledge that every whole—including individual words—is composed of parts, and directed study of those parts can help a student to master the whole. Experience and research tell us that regular attention to phonics, other word attack skills, spelling, etc., develops reading mastery, thereby completing the unity of the whole language experience. The child is thus led to read, write, spell, speak, and listen confidently in response to a literature experience introduced by the teacher. In these ways, language skills grow rapidly, stimulated by direct practice, involvement, and interest in the topic at hand.

Why Thematic Planning?

A whole language program is best implemented with thematic planning. The teacher plans classroom activities correlated to specific literature selections, and centered around a predetermined theme. Students tend to learn and retain more when they are applying their skills in an interesting and meaningful context. Both teachers and students will be freed from a day that is broken into unrelated segments of isolated drill and practice.

Why Cooperative Learning?

Students need to learn social appropriateness, as well as academic skills. This area of development cannot be taken for granted. Because group activities are a part of living, it is important to consider social objectives in your planning. Students working together will select leaders and designate responsibilities within their groups. The teacher is present to explain social goals and monitor interaction.

Why Make Books?

Groups of children may produce a book as a cooperative learning project. In so doing, they gain experience in reading, writing, spelling, and illustrating. In this unit, student-made books help teach a skill or recall a story and can become part of the classroom library to be read and reread.

These books make excellent culminating projects for sharing beyond the classroom with parents, librarians, and other classrooms. This unit contains specific directions for three of the many methods to produce big books.

Cars and Trucks and Things That Go

by Richard Scarry

Summary

The young reader travels along through delightful pictures and words as the Pig family takes a drive to a picnic at the beach. Along the way, they pass a construction site, military base, car fire, farm, ski resort, airport, and railroad station. They see real and imaginary vehicles. Upon arriving home, Ma and Pa surprise Penny and Pickles with a toy car of their own.

Concepts

- There are many different things that go.
- Trucks are at work in the environment.
- Trucks are used to transport goods.
- Vehicles are used by community workers.

Suggested Activities

— List vehicles in the book. **Categorize** them as land, air, water. Use the same categories to make a picture chart of magazine/newspaper cutouts.

— Encourage students to **search** for vehicles at work as they travel around town with their families **and share** their findings with the class. Discuss the Roadwork Machines and the kind of work they do, page 13.

— Plan **a field trip** to see one of the following up close: fire truck, police car, ambulance, mail truck, city bus, construction vehicles, etc.

— Make and use the Vocabulary and Picture Cards on pages 7–8 for matching, making sentences that emphasize these concepts, and for other **creative writing activities**.

— Encourage young children to **observe and count** the various types, sizes, and colors in cars and trucks while traveling with their families, pages 7, 8, 11, 17, 19 and 20. Remind students that color words are on the color markers.

— Make a Panel Big Book of Things That Go, page 22.

— Have any of the children traveled in a motorhome? (page 21) Invite them to share magazine pictures or family photos.

— Write original stories titled If I Had a Dump Truck. Younger students may draw the truck's load, page 10.

— As you read, look for **alliteration** in the names of the characters— Rollo Rabbit, Paul the Painter, Dingo Dog, Mistress Mouse, etc. Use this as a mini lesson on initial consonant sounds. Try assigning similar names to your students.

Cars and Trucks and Things That Go (cont.)

— Encourage students to locate and discuss real and imaginary vehicles. In which vehicles have the students ridden? Make the wheel mobiles (page 56), adding their own creation to it.

— Make back-to-back charts to summarize what you have learned.

What trucks carry	What trucks do
grain	dig ditches
logs	lay pipes
molasses	push dirt
hay	crush rocks

— Discuss the places in the story and help Officer Flossy catch Dingo Dog in the Maze, page 12.

— Suggest **similar locations** in your community. Are you near a ski resort, army base, golf course, airport, or road construction? What do you think happened to Dingo Dog when he was caught by Officer Flossy? Use the Street Playmat on page 73 to role play the scene.

— Share the poetry on page 49. Make lists of **word families** (endings) using car, boat, and van. Use the rhyming word lists to help in writing a couplet at the bottom of page 49. Send it home to be enjoyed!

— Make a Train Flip Book on page 53. Fill it with goods that are transported by train. If there is a train crossing near your school, discuss **safety concerns**.

— Assemble the cut-and-paste pick-up truck from **shapes** on page 59. Can children name each shape? Fill the bed of the truck with a load cut from magazine pictures. Share it with the class.

— Discuss road and vehicle **safety**, stressing the need for seat belts in all vehicles, page 67. Ask students to look for road signs on their way to school. Take a walk and practice obeying traffic lights when crossing the street. Complete the activity using pages 68–69.

— Is there heavy snow where you live? **Write a letter** explaining snowmobiles and snowblowers to children living in warm climates. Tell what you do on snow days when there is no school.

— **Share other related stories** from Richard Scary's *What Do People Do All Day? Firemen to the Rescue, The Train Trip, Building a New Road,* and *A Voyage on a Ship.*

— Activity pages 15–16, 20, 57–60 all **relate math** to our travel unit. Play the Parking Lot Game on page 55.

Vocabulary and Picture Cards

car	
truck	
bus	
train	
bike	

Vocabulary and Picture Cards *(cont.)*

	plane
	helicopter
	sailboat
	rowboat
	ship

8

Color Words

1. Read the color words.
2. Color each car with its color.

3. Cut out the car boxes.
4. Glue cars on the carrier by color.

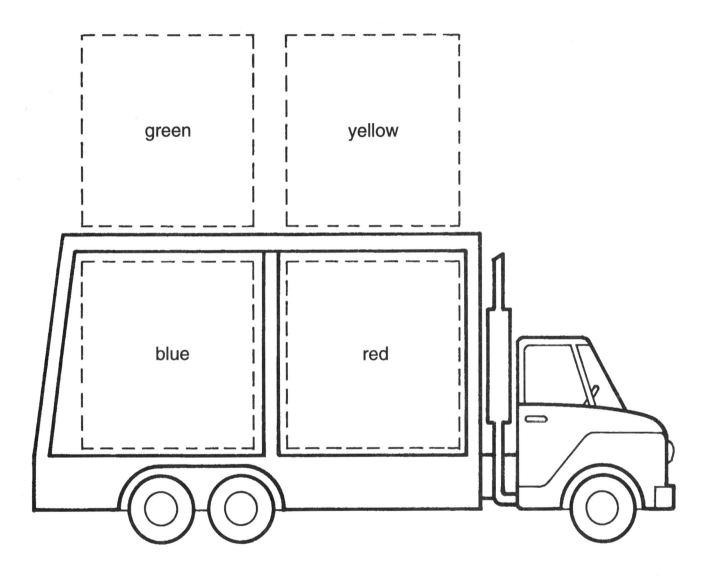

green

yellow

blue

red

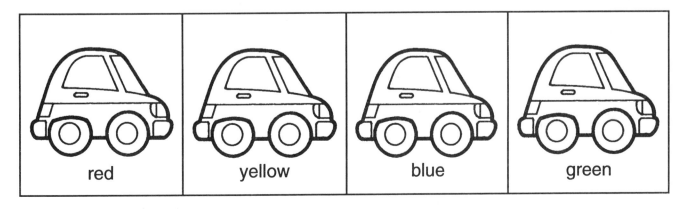

red

yellow

blue

green

Dump Trucks

1. Read the story.
2. Draw the truck driver's load.

3. Color the picture.
4. Finish the sentence below.

The driver has dumped his load of_____.

Design a Car or Truck

1. Finish drawing a funny car or truck.
2. Draw yourself in the seat driving.

3. Give it a funny name.
4. Fill in the story blanks below.

This is a_____.   It is a_____.
　　　　　　　　　　　　　　　　　　　　　　　(car / truck)

It can go _____.   It is _____.
　　　　　(fast / slow)　　　　　　　　　　　　　(big / little)

It has four _____ and two _____.
　　　　　　(wheels / doors)　　　　　　　　　　　(wheels / doors)

Its color is _____.   It is _____!
(The color word is on your marker or crayon.)　　　(super/great/silly)

Maze

Help Officer Flossy catch Dingo Dog!

1. Follow the road with your pencil.
2. Color Goldbug yellow.

3. Color Officer Flossy blue.
4. Color Dingo green.

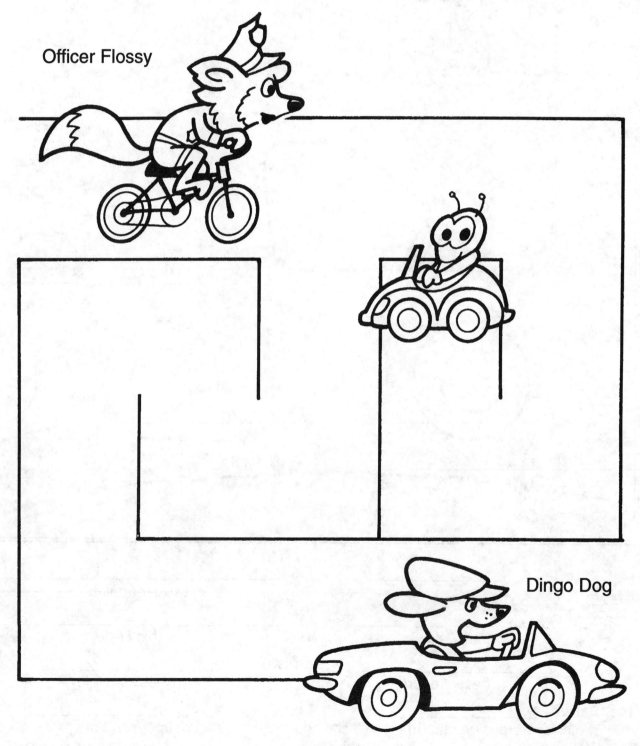

Officer Flossy

Dingo Dog

Roadwork Machines

These machines help people build roads. What does each machine do?

1. Choose words from the
   Word Bank below.

2. Write your answers on the
   line under each picture.

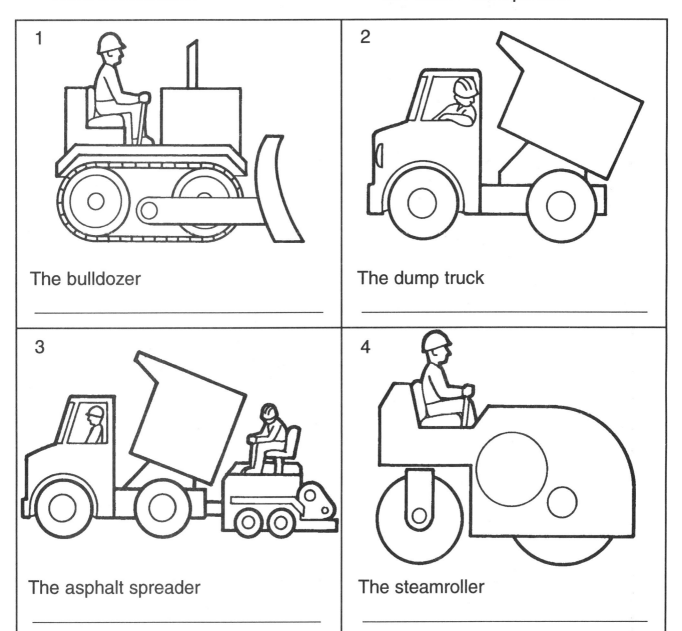

1

The bulldozer
_____

2

The dump truck
_____

3

The asphalt spreader
_____

4

The steamroller
_____

Word Bank

___ moves dirt. ___ carries gravel. ___ spreads asphalt. ___ flattens the road.

3. Now cut out the boxes.

4. Staple them into a book.

5. Color the pictures.

6. Read it to everyone!

Painter's Pickup

Peter Painter needs your help brightening his truck with color.

1. Color his truck and the paint cans. Watch for the color words!
2. Cut out the boxed paint cans below.
3. Glue the cans in the back of the truck.

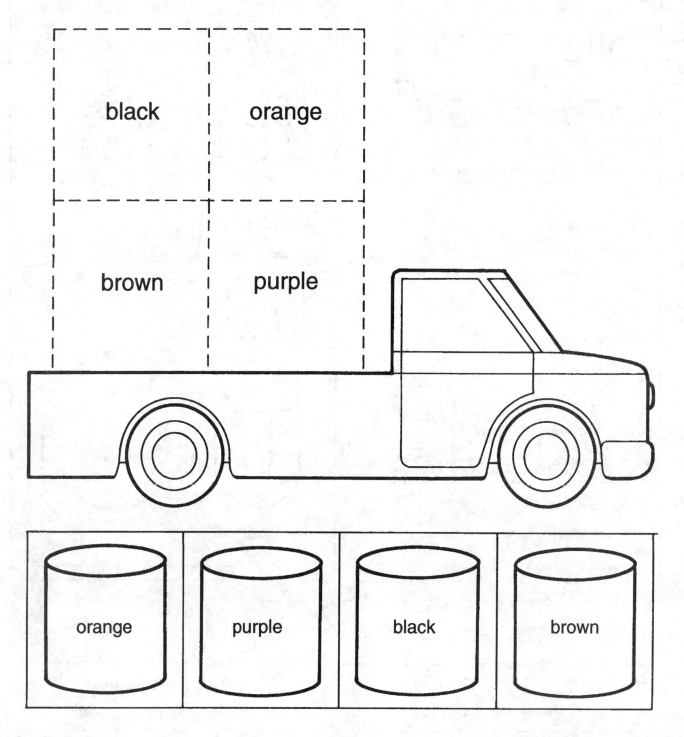

Watermelon Wagon and Flying Fish

Follow the directions:

---

1. Count how many fish. _____

   You draw one more.

   Write how many now. _____

---

2. Count how many watermelons. _____

   You draw one more.

   Write how many now. _____

   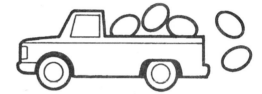

---

3. Count how many fish. _____

   You draw one more.

   Write how many now. _____

---

4. Count how many watermelons. _____

   You draw one more.

   Write how many now. _____

---

5. Count how many fish. _____

   You draw one more.

   Write how many now. _____

---

6. Count how many watermelons. _____

   You draw one more.

   Write how many now. _____

   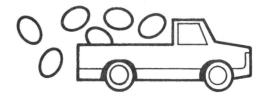

Count and Draw

1. Write how many suitcases.

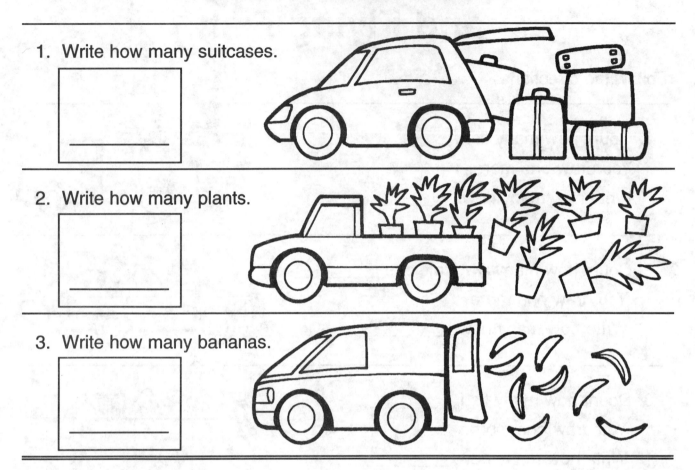

2. Write how many plants.

3. Write how many bananas.

4. Draw 5 watermelons.

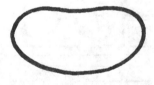

5. Draw 9 ears of corn.

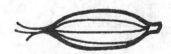

6. Draw 7 paint cans.

Trucks Carry Many Things

1. Cut out the door and the truck.

2. Match the truck to its name.

3. Glue the top edge of the door to the truck.

4. Color the open truck and the door.

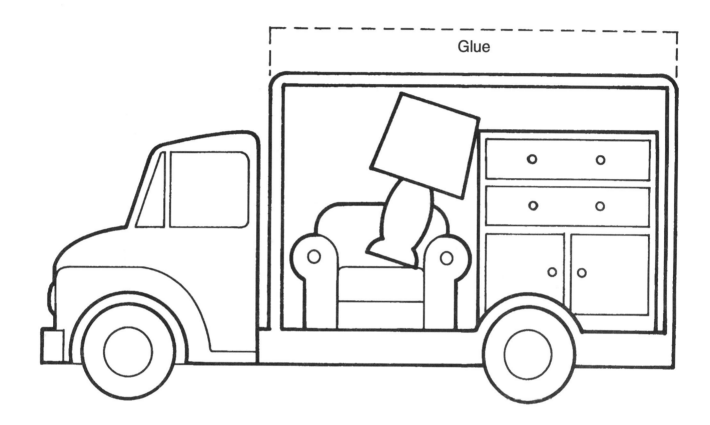

Glue

truck door

MISSY'S MOVERS

Trucks Carry Many Things *(cont.)*

1. Cut out the door and the truck.

2. Match the truck to its name.

3. Glue the top edge of the door to the truck.

4. Color the open truck and the door.

Glue

truck door

Fred's
Farm
Foods

Trucks Carry Many Things *(cont.)*

1. Cut out the door and the truck.

2. Match the truck to its name.

3. Glue the top edge of the door to the truck.

4. Color the open truck and the door.

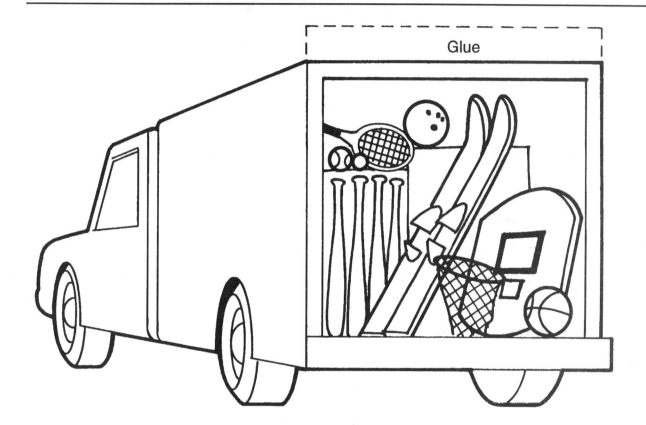

Glue

truck door

Sam's Sports Store

Cars and Trucks . . .

Racing Cars

All the cars are going fast! Use the number words below to show who was first, second, third, fourth, fifth, and sixth.

1. Color the cars and the racetrack.

2. Cut out the number word boxes below.

3. Glue the correct label to show how each car placed in the race.

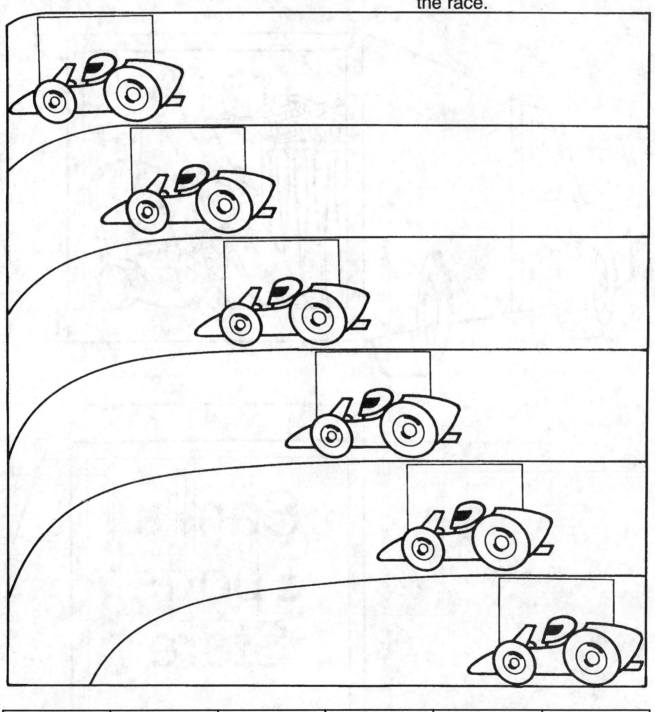

| first | second | third | fourth | fifth | sixth |

20

Molly's Motorhome

Molly is going on a long, long trip. She is taking everything with her!

1. Draw what you think should be inside of her motorhome (top picture).
2. Color both pictures and cut them out.
3. Glue the outside like a flap across the inside motorhome.
4. Write a short story on the back of the lifted flap.

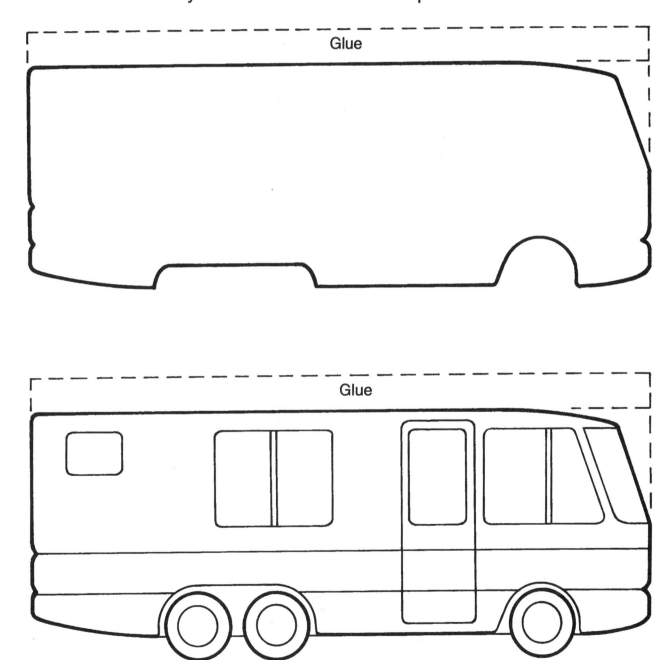

Panel Big Book

1. Cut a 12-foot (3.6 m) length of white tag board or butcher paper.

2. Accordion fold the paper into four sections.

3. Spread the paper out on the floor so the children can have access to draw directly on it, or they can glue on large pictures that they drew and cut out.

4. Some of the vehicles your students may want to draw are:

van	rowboat	truck	airplane	motorhome
bus	houseboat	blimp	rocket	motorcycle
ship	sailboat	train	helicopter	bicycle

Students may wish to categorize their pictures: land, air, water. Label each page with the vehicle name. Where appropriate, ask children to dictate (or write) original sentences for their pictures, naming each picture and telling what each vehicle does.

5. Display the finished project as a mural. Practice reading the text and labels.

6. Fold the mural on the original accordion folds. Staple it close to the left edge. Tape over staples to prevent cuts and to lengthen the life of the book.

7. If you decide to let students take the book home to share with their parents, you might add another last page for parents to write positive notes about the book to the class. Students love it! And parents will enjoy reading it again as well as all the comments, if you save it to display at the next Parents' Night at school.

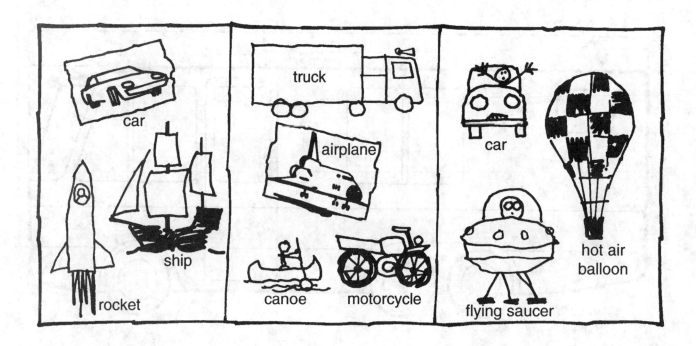

Opposites

1. Read the sentence.
2. Look at the picture.

3. Circle the correct word or words.
4. Color each picture the correct color.

Pigs are _____ a red car.

in   out of

Pigs are _____ the black car.

in   out of

This blue car is _____.

up   down

This pink car is _____.

up   down

His green bike is _____.

fast   slow

Her yellow bike is _____.

fast   slow

This brown car is _____.

old   new

This orange car is _____.

old   new

Where Does It Go?

1. Print the correct word from below.   2. Draw the correct picture.

1. _____

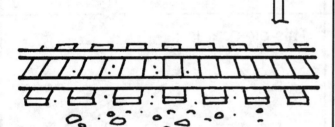

2. _____

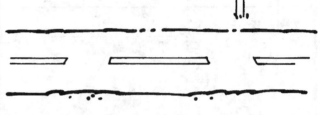

3. _____

4. _____

Word Bank: train   car   plane   boat

First Flight

by David McPhail

Summary

A young child takes his first flight to visit his grandma. While he boards the plane, his only companion, a teddy bear, comes to life. The boy is a model passenger. It is the bear who encounters difficulties in this humorous high-flying adventure that teaches us a lot about air travel along the way.

Concepts

- The airlines need many different people to do jobs.
- Air travel is very different from forms of ground travel.
- It is important to follow safety rules.

Suggested Activities

— **Brainstorm:** 1. a list of reasons why people might take a plane trip, 2. what they might take along other than their luggage, and 3. what foods they might get on the plane (page 32). Share students' experiences on airplanes and encourage them to role play and then dictate or write their own stories (real or make-believe).

— **List airline** jobs from the pictures in the book—ticket agent, security guard, baggage handler, flight attendant, captain—and the basic job training that might be needed. Make Lift-the-Flap Book, pages 35–38.

— If it is possible, arrange a **class trip** to an airport near you. Look also for workers who were not included in the story. Have students make picture stories about airline workers.

— Make a Venn diagram **comparing/contrasting** air and ground travel.

— Ask students who have flown to **share their stories** (orally, written, or dictated) and discuss what is best about each form of travel.

— Discuss **safety measures** that were shown in the story and what happens if rules are not followed. Stress the importance of seat belts in car, air, and boat travel, page 67.

— Discuss what is done **behind the scenes** to prepare the plane for flight. **Make inferences** from information in the story.

— Make a **graph** showing how your students travel to visit their grandparents. Which ones must take a plane flight?

— Teach **telephone etiquette** for calling friends and relatives. In cooperative groups, brainstorm ideas. Report back to the whole group. Then in pairs, role play calling grandparents about the upcoming trip. Encourage students to write about the experience. Then evaluate how their small group did, page 27.

— Play this version of an old favorite **game**, "I'm going to Grandma's and I'm going to take . . ." Discuss packing for a trip, and complete the work sheet on page 28.

First Flight *(cont.)*

— Air travel has a special **vocabulary**: pilot, airplane, ticket, suitcase runway, turbulence, cabin, baggage, cockpit, flight attendant, terminal, security, passenger, captain. Discuss these words and complete the work sheet on page 39.

— Make the **Paper Bag Bear** on page 29. Role play in pairs and small groups for the next three activities. Allow students to take their Paper Bag Bears home to use for sharing their stories with their families.

— Discuss the boy's and the bear's **emotions** during their first flight. Why did they experience such a range of feelings? How might the flight have been different without the bear? Complete the worksheet on page 31. Invite students to write their own stories about an imaginary friend, page 30.

— Invite students to share their experiences eating on a plane—kinds of foods, how they were served, foods they probably would and would **not** get to eat there. Then complete page 32 by drawing the foods and **writing a menu** below it from a word bank that the teacher writes on the board.

— **Rewrite** the story from the bear's point of view. Bind the story in a class book with a teddy bear-shaped cover. Allow students to check it out to take home for family enjoyment, encouraging parents' comments on a blank last page.

— Practice **folding airplanes** (page 63). Decorate them. Take them to the playground to fly.

— Make a **glider** (page 61). Practice flying the gliders through a suspended hula hoop or into a large target marked on the classroom floor.

— For more specific information about air travel, share a **nonfiction** book like My *Lift-the-Flap Plane Book* by Angela Royston, G. P. Putnam & Sons, 1993. Complete the lift-the-flap book on pages 35–38.

— Complete the work sheet "I'm Going on an Airplane" on page 34 by filling in the **initial consonants** for the words in both the top and the bottom of the page. Read the story.

— Recall the events of the story in order with the **sequencing** worksheet on page 33. Have the children cut the boxes apart and glue them in order onto construction paper.

— **Write a sequel** to this story with the boy telling his grandmother about the flight. In pairs, The boy and his grandmother might reenact the trip by pretending the various parts of the trip.

— Make each child a set of small **captain's wings** from yellow tagboard. Glue a safety pin to the back so that students can wear them home.

A Call to a Grandparent

In pairs, role-play a telephone call to your grandma and grandpa. Remember that conversation is a happy sharing about what is happening in your lives.

1. Greet them with a smile in your voice.
2. Ask about them and their activities.
3. Share your activities and interests.
4. Talk about doing something together.
5. Write about your conversation below.

Cooperative group check-up:

6. We did well when . . . _____

_____

7. We need to work on . . . _____

_____

Packing for My Trip

Draw at least four things you would pack for a plane trip to your grandma's.

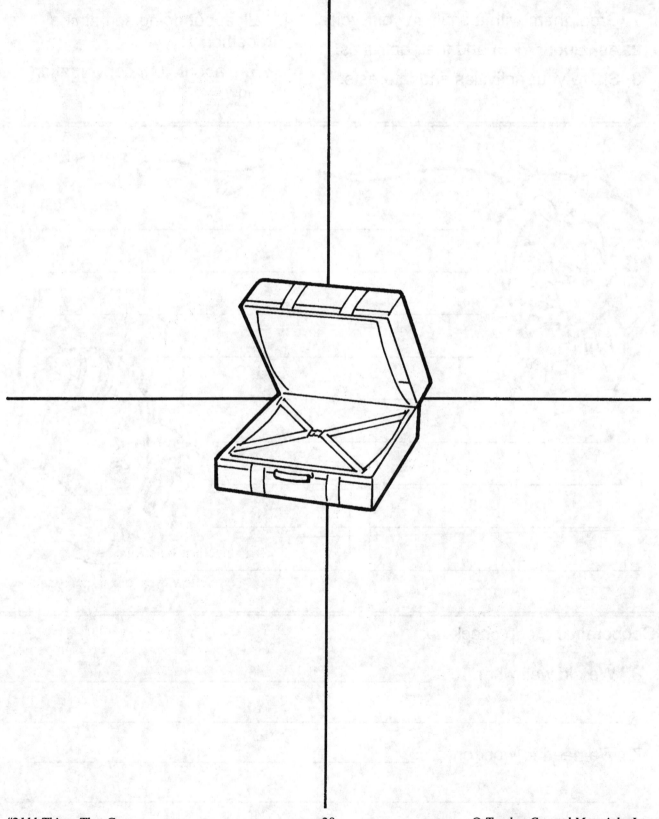

Paper Bag Bear

You will need:

- 2 large paper grocery bags
- 4 brown paper lunch bags
- several plastic trash bags (or other stuffing material)
- construction paper scraps (brown, yellow, and pink)
- black marker
- masking tape and glue

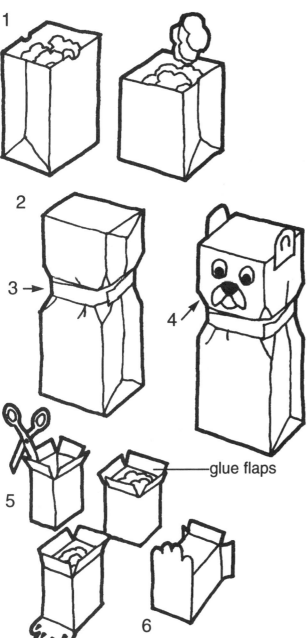

glue flaps

Directions:

1. Crumble stuffing inside the two large bags.

2. Invert one bag inside the other.

3. Tape together at neckline.

4. Glue on yellow eyes, a pink nose, and brown ears.

5. For arms and legs: cut glue flaps about 1" (4 cm) down from the top on each corner of the small lunch bag. Stuff.

6. Glue on four pink paper paws. Draw the claws.

7. Tape the finished arms and legs onto the bear's body.

My Imaginary Friend

1. In the top space draw a picture of you and your imaginary friend doing something on the plane.

2. Write your story about the picture on the lines below. Read the story to your friends and family.

_____

_____

_____

_____

_____

In Flight Feelings

1. Choose two words from the Word Bank. Write one word under each picture.

2. Draw that kind of face.

3. Finish the picture. Color it.

4. Write a story on the back.

Word Bank: sad   happy   sleepy   hungry   relaxed   uncomfortable

A Meal on the Plane

1. Draw your favorite airplane meal in the top space.
2. Write a menu of the foods you drew in the bottom space.
3. Cut out the menu.
4. Glue it like a flap over your food tray.

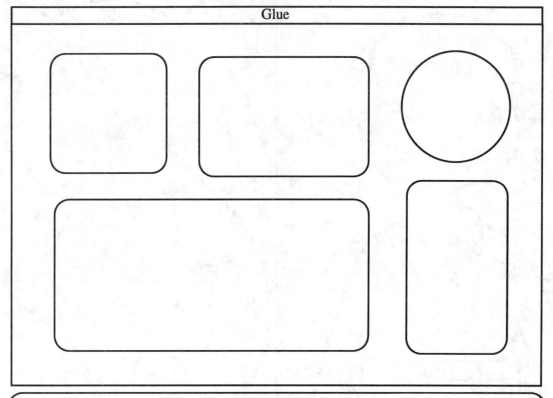

Menu

My Favorite Airplane Meal

_____

_____

_____

_____

_____

_____

_____

Story Sequence

1. Number the pictures in the order they happened.
2. Cut the boxes apart.
3. Glue the boxes in correct order onto construction paper.
4. Color the pictures in.

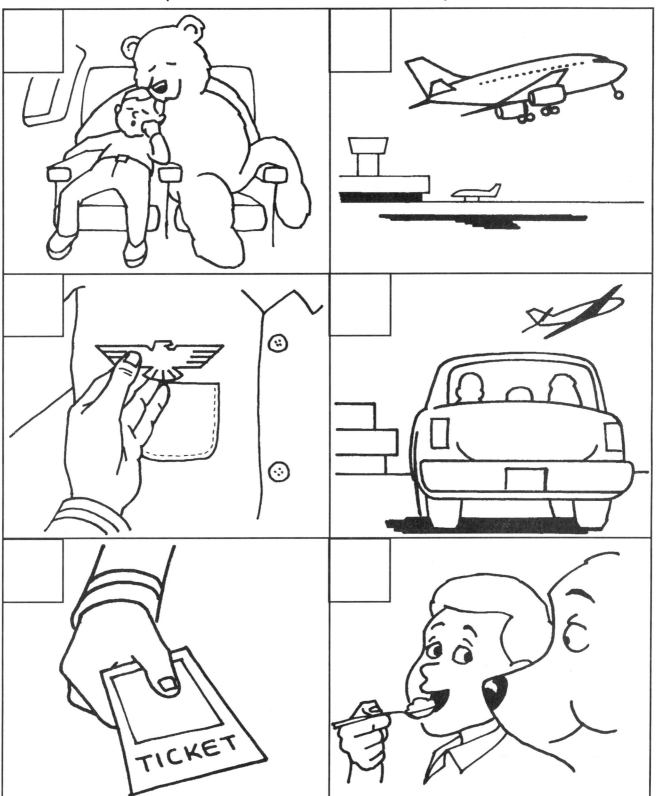

I'm Going on an Airplane!

1. Write the missing letter for each picture.
2. Write the missing letters in the story below.

Letter Bank			
b	c	l	m
p	s	t	w

   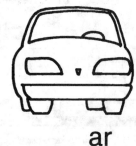      

_____ icket   _____ ar   _____ ear   _____ lane

_____ uitcase   _____ovie   _____ ings   _____ unch

I'm Going on an Airplane!

I got my ___uitcase.   We took a ___ar to the airport.   I got a ___icket.

My ___ear got big.   We went on a big ___lane.

We ate ___unch.

We saw a funny ___ovie.

The captain gave me gold flight ___ings.

It was a great trip!

Lift-the-Flap Book

1. Read and talk about pages 35, 36, 37 and 38.

2. Cut the pages and flaps apart.

3. Glue the flaps to the correct picture.

4. Staple the pages together in number order.

5. Glue your school photo to the title page face. Color all the pictures.

6. Share your book with your family and friends.

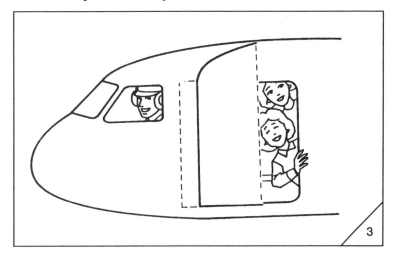

3

Lift-the-Flap Book

Come, Fly With Me!

1

Lift-the-Flap Book *(cont.)*

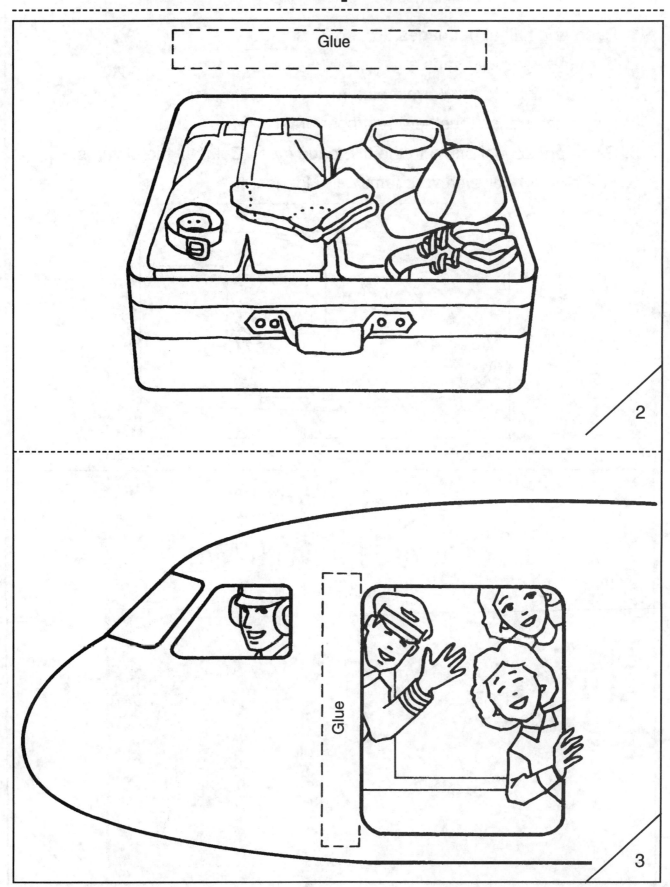

Glue

2

Glue

3

36

Lift-the-Flap Book *(cont.)*

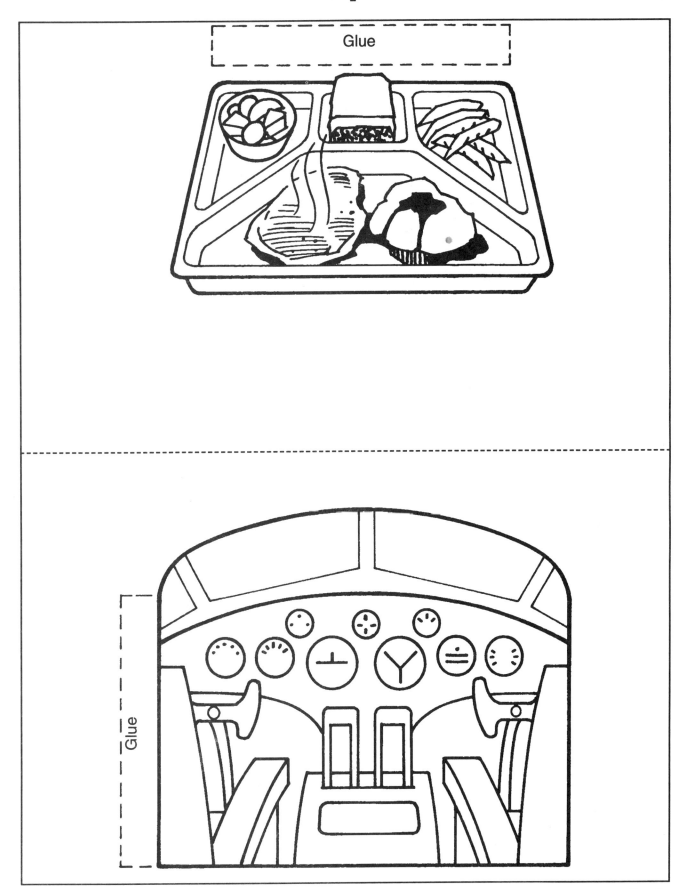

Glue

Glue

Lift-the-Flap Book *(cont.)*

Flaps

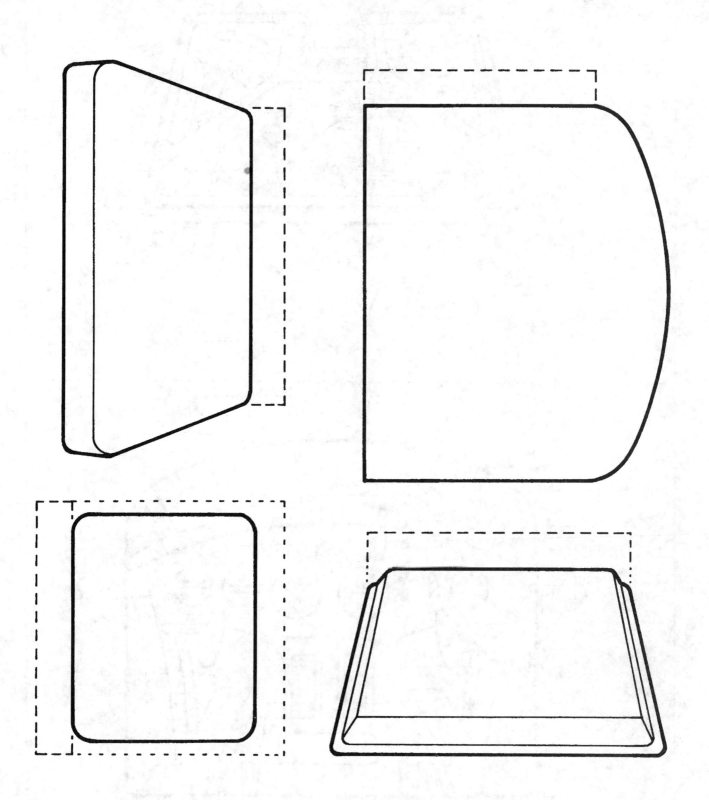

38

Airport Words

1. Say the words.
2. Match the words to the pictures.

3. Cut out the word boxes.
4. Glue them to the correct picture.

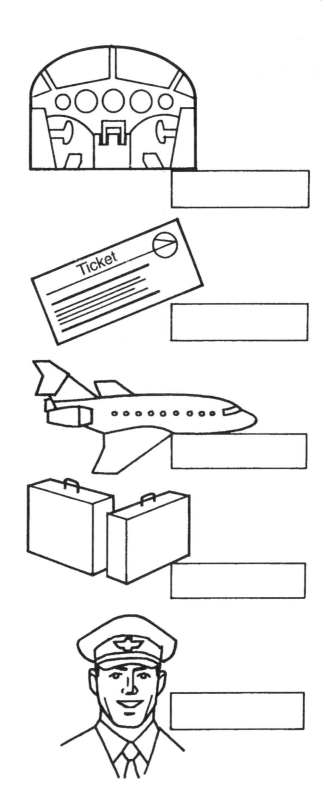

ticket

cockpit

airplane

pilot

2 suitcases

Big City Port

by Betsy Maestro and Ellen Del Vecchio

Summary

All types of boats come into the busy seaport. They are unloaded by dock workers using a variety of equipment. The captain of the port, as well as the harbor police and fireboats, keep things running smoothly.

Concepts

- There are many different kinds of boats.
- Each kind of boat does a different job.
- The seaport is busy all day and all night.

Suggested Activities:

— Allow children to share their experience with boats. **Brainstorn** what they already know.

— Make a **chart** showing the name, job, simple description, and small picture of the different boats discussed in the book.

— Make word/picture/job description cards for **categorizing** boats.

— Discuss how the **size and shape** of the boat is a factor in the job it does. Explain the work of a tugboat. Complete the worksheet on page 44.

— Cut boxes, barrels, and bales from construction paper. Use them for **counting and graphing** activities. Discuss what products might be carried inside each container. Complete the Dock Scene worksheet page 45.

— **List** the workers pictured in the book. **Discuss good and bad aspects** of working on the docks.

— **Compare/contrast** the day and night activities at the port. Discuss a fisherman's day from the time he leaves the port in the morning until his return at night. Complete the **Opposites** work sheet on page 43.

— Look at a **map** of the United States and determine major seaports. The teacher can stick "Post-its" labeled with Los Angeles, Long Beach, San Francisco, Boston, Miami, New York, New Orleans, and Houston in the correct places.

— Collect travel brochures from several cruise lines. Make a **graph** showing the students who have taken a cruise, or interview someone who has been on a cruise. Mark the departure points on a map. Have students put together the Ocean Liner **Puzzle,** page 42. Prepare several other boat picture puzzles to use in a learning center.

— If you live near a seaport, invite a dock worker to be a **speaker** to your class, or arrange a class **field trip** to see the workers firsthand.

Big City Port *(cont.)*

— Share the books *Harbor* by Donald Crews, Greenwillow, 1982, and *Boat Book* by Gail Gibbons, Holiday House, 1983, for **more information** about a variety of boats.

— Make a Tugboat/Barge, page 65, to conduct small group **"float or sink" experiments**. First try to guess the results. Have the class vote tallied in columns 1. Record in column 2 how the experiment turned out for each student. Circle the results to show whether each floated or sank.

— Make the sailboats, on page 64 and allow students to continue the **"float/sail" experiment**.

— **Brainstorm** a list of water safety rules for both swimming and boating. Stress the importance of learning to swim. Allow students to share the fun of it. Write them on a chart.

— **Compare/contrast** harbor police and firemen with city police and firefighters on both land and water.

— What do you hear in a garage? Have children act out **Garage Sounds**. Let them think of others (squeal, thunk, chug-chug, hum . . .). To show an understanding of each word, let students match words to sounds they might hear in a garage, on page 50.

— Complete the What's Inside the Boat? worksheet on page 47. Extend it to other forms of transportation by **questioning** what might be inside various kinds of trains, planes, and vehicles.

— Teach your students the **map directions**: *north, south, east,* and *west*. Mark the directions on the walls of your classroom. Play **The Direction Game**. One child is "It." (blindfolded) Students "sail" into port by moving to one of the directional signs. "It" calls out one direction. Children in that port "go home" (sit down). At the end, the student left standing gets to be "It" for the next round. Complete the worksheet Boats Come Into Port on page 46.

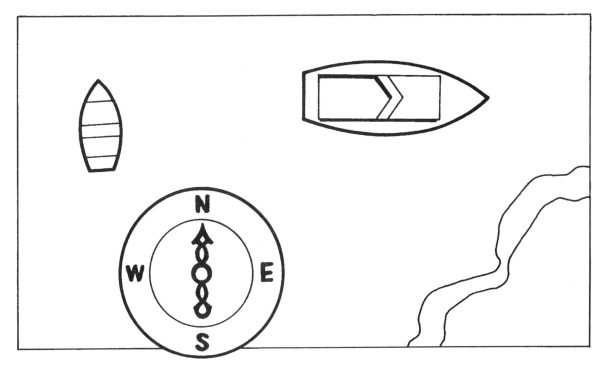

Ocean Liner Puzzle

1. Cut out the puzzle pieces.

2. Place the puzzle pieces to make a ship.

3. Glue the ship to a blue paper ocean.

4. Color the ocean liner.

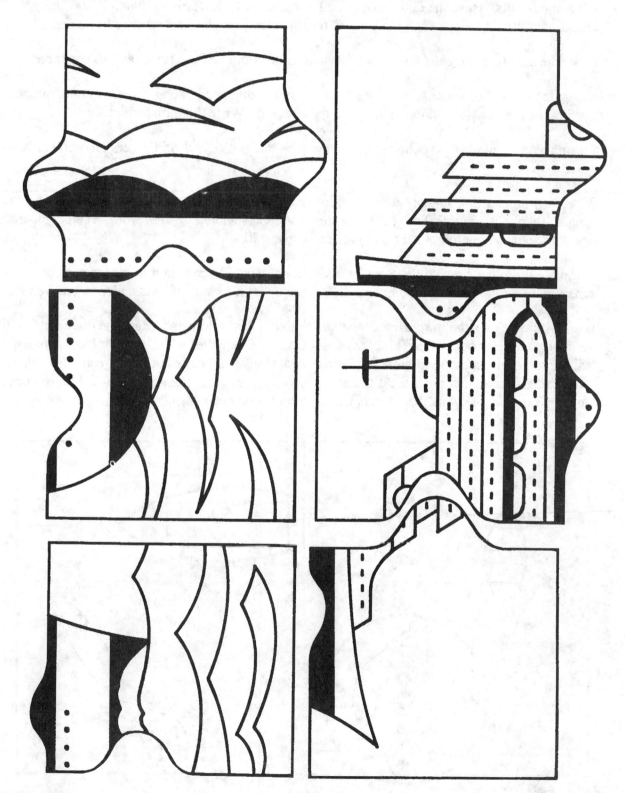

42

Opposites

1. Say the words. Work across.
2. Circle the words that are opposites

3. Draw the opposite.
4. On the back draw more opposites.

See the (morning) (sun.)	See the (evening) (moon.)
This boat's sails are up.	This boat's sails are down.
What a big ocean liner!	What a little tugboat!
I go on land.	I go on water.

Tugboat

1. Color each tugboat piece at the bottom with a different color.
2. Cut out just the bottom four tugboat pieces.
3. Glue those four pieces to the tugboat at the top.
4. Color the water around the little tugboat.

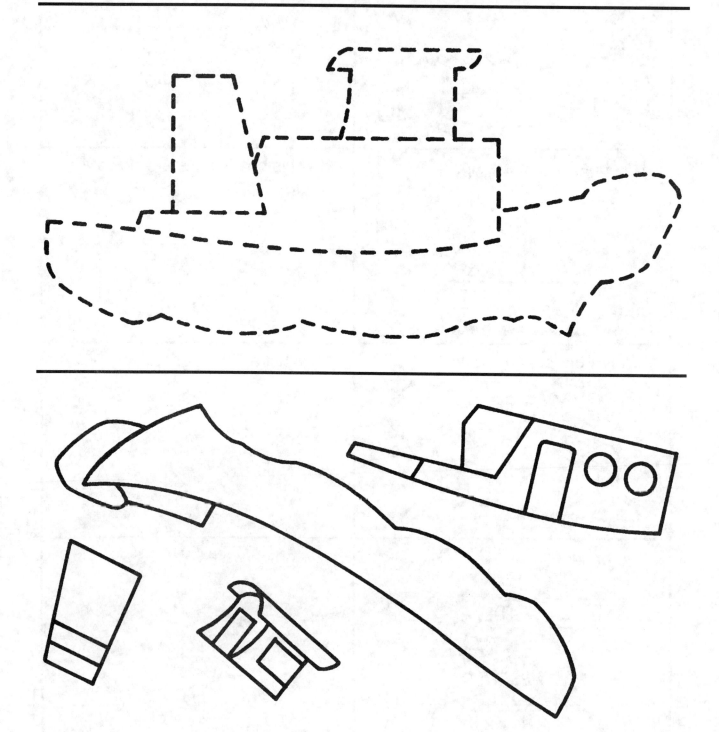

Dock Scene

1. Pretend you are a dock worker.

2. Load this cargo by drawing
   in a good spot the number of things
   listed on the right.

Draw:

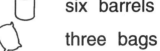

four boxes

five bales

six barrels

three bags

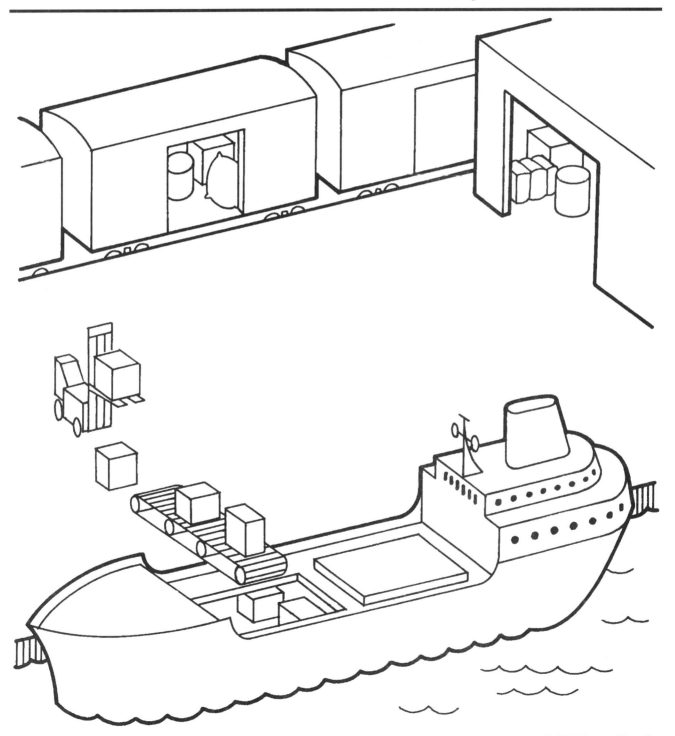

Boats Come Into Port

Directions: Direct boats which way to go. A compass helps us to find our direction. The compass direction points are **north**, **south**, **east**, and **west**.

1. Color the boat dock, the four boats below, and the ocean water.

2. Cut out the little boats and sail them safely home.

3. Glue each boat at its correct spot. Is it north, south, east, or west?

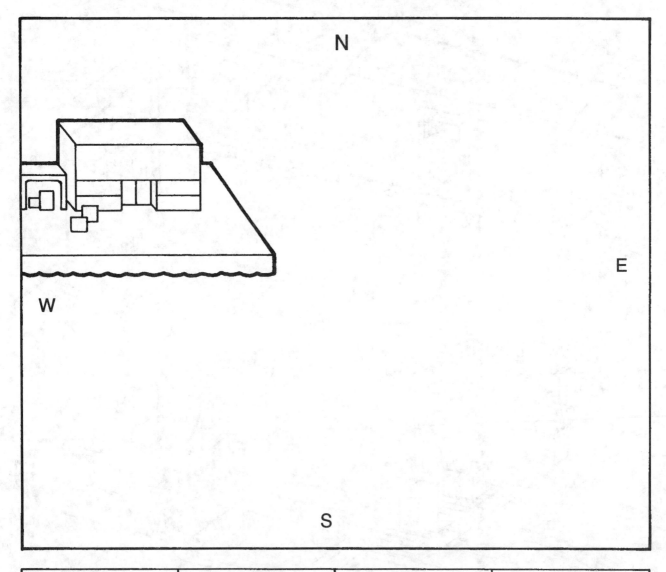

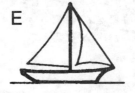
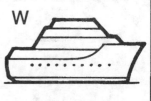

What's Inside the Boat?

Match the words to the correct pictures.

ocean liner

fishing boat

ferry boat

cargo freighter

fireboat

oil tanker

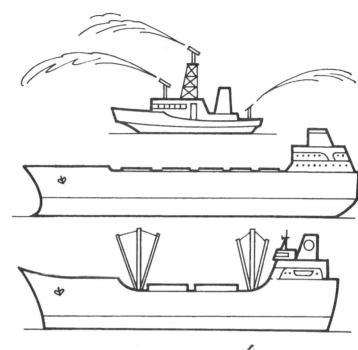

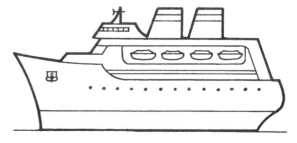

Sew a Sailboat

You can learn while you sew!

1. Use a shoe string to connect the dots by sewing in and out.

2. Practice sewing by counting from 1 to 10 on the sails and the boat.

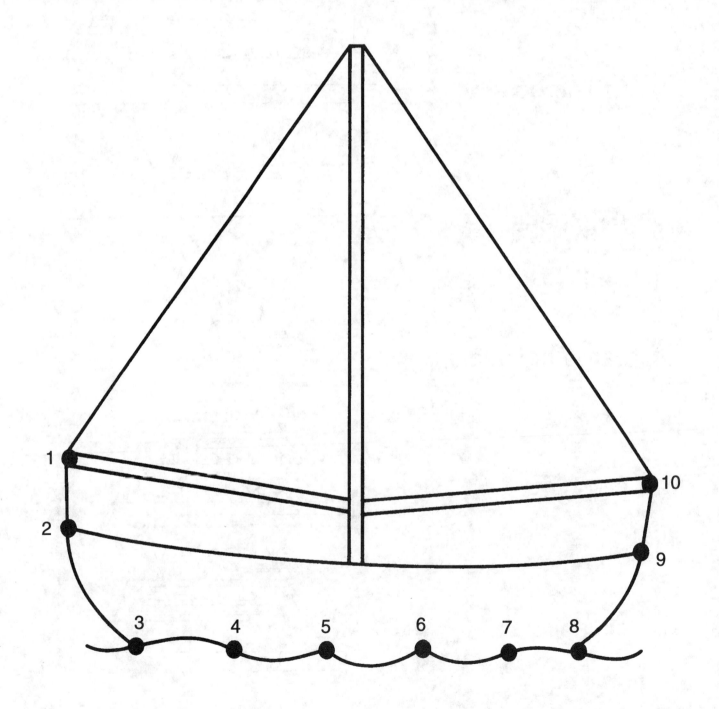

48

Poetry

On the Go

Cars go fast and cars go slow
All around our town,
While over at the airport
The planes go up and down.
The boats out in the harbor
Seem to rest all day.
One day soon the wind will blow
And they will sail away.

Flight

I'd like to take a plane flight
High up in the sky.
I'd look out of my window
And watch the world go by.

Truck

Truck,
Long, shiny,
Rolling, hauling, honking,
Moving down the road.
18-wheeler!

My Bike

Best thing I have.
I love how it feels!
Kids' transportation,
Everyday wheels.

• •

Travel Bug

When I first learned to walk around
I always loved to go!
But pretty soon I realized
My feet were kind of slow.
Then I learned to roller skate
And found out how it feels
To zoom along the sidewalk
On feet dressed up in wheels.

Sometimes I think I'd like to own
A train all shiny black.
My friends would all come running,
And we'd chug on down the track.
Now you may choose to go by plane,
But there's one thing I know.
When you catch that "travel bug"
You'll always love to go!

A poem can be just 2 lines. Write your poem here.

_____

_____

Garage Sounds

What could make these sounds?

1. Say the sounds that the words make.

2. Draw lines to match each word to its picture.

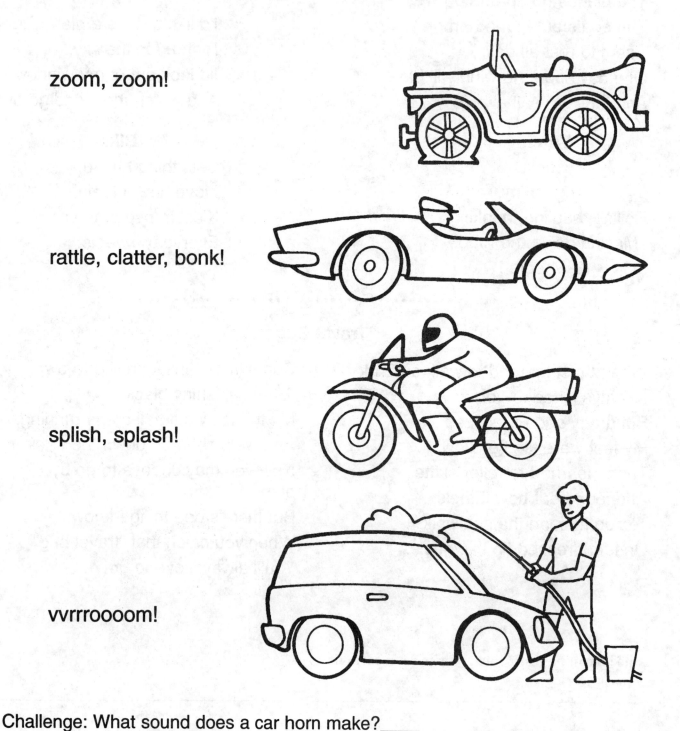

zoom, zoom!

rattle, clatter, bonk!

splish, splash!

vvrrrooooom!

Challenge: What sound does a car horn make?____ ____ ____ ____

Wheel Book

What you need:

- wheels reproduced onto two pieces of 9" x 12" (23 cm x 31 cm) construction paper
- color markers
- scissors
- 1 paper fastener (brad)

What you do:

1. Cut around the two wheels for the front and back covers, page 52.

2. From the front wheel-shaped cover, cut out one pie section.

3. Join the front wheel to the back wheel through the center dot with the paper fastener.

4. Begin with the cut opening at the bottom right. Draw and label or write your story on the back wheel-shaped cover, moving to the right, one pie section at a time.

5. Continue moving the wheel to the right, filling in all six sections.

6. Number the pictures and words in order.

7. Share your book with a friend!

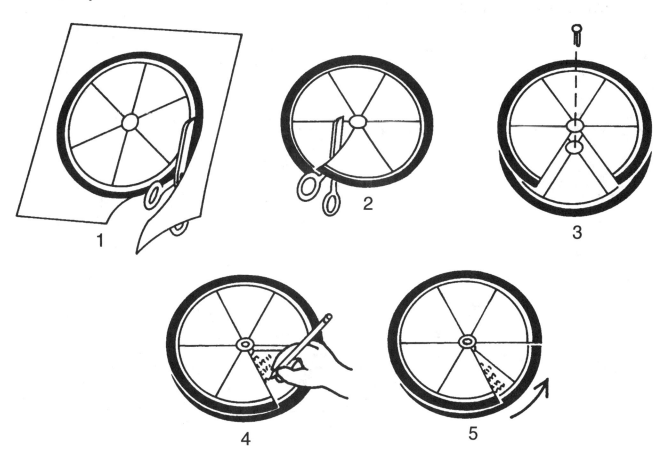

Wheel Book *(cont.)*

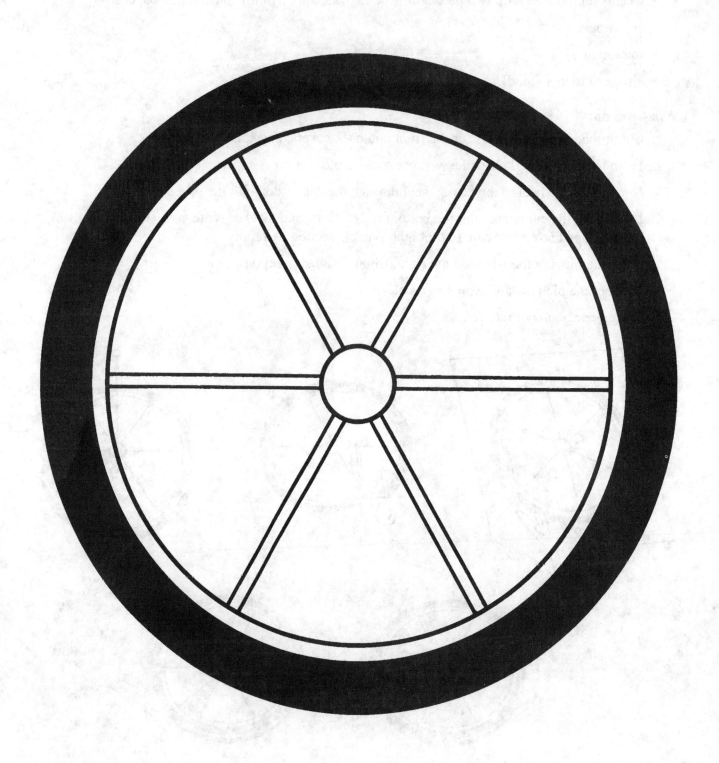

Train Flip Book

What you need:

- 1 piece 9" x 12" (23 cm x 31 cm) construction paper, folded in half lengthwise and marked in thirds

- paper scraps for wheels

- 1 copy of train engine pattern (page 54)

- color markers

- scissors

- glue

What you do:

1. Color and cut out the train engine.

2. Fold the construction paper in half lengthwise.

3. Cut **only the top** into three flaps, as shown below.

4. Under each flap, write a different sentence: _____ go on trains. (circus animals, kinds of cars, kinds of foods, kinds of building materials, etc.) Draw a picture of each.

5. Cut out three wheels.

6. Glue them onto the front flaps of the train cars.

7. Glue the engine onto the front of the train.

Train Flip Book *(cont.)*

Engine Pattern

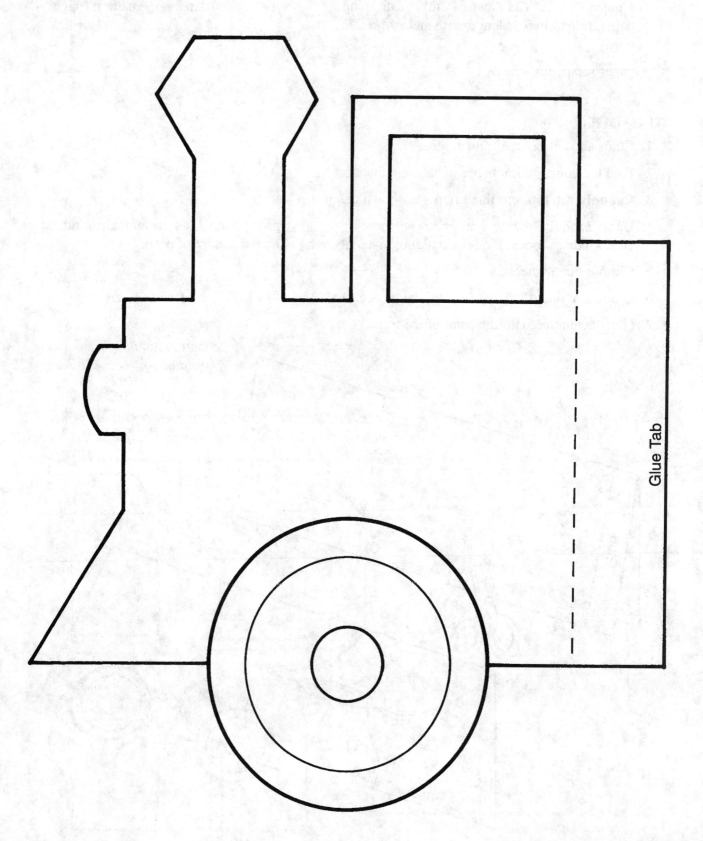

Glue Tab

54

Parking Lot Game

Materials:

- a sturdy cardboard box with a lid about 9" x 12" (23 cm x 31 cm)
- a small box about 3" x 4" (8 cm x 10 cm)
- two sets of the patterns (below)
- tagboard
- one sheet gray construction paper 9" x 12" (23 cm x 31 cm)

- color markers
- glue
- ruler
- sharp scissors, sharp knife
- masking tape

Directions:

1. **Make the game pieces.** Copy two sets of the cards (see below). Determine the skill for your game. Add words and pictures or numerals and sets to the vehicles. Color the pictures and glue them to tagboard. Laminate all the pieces. Cut around the shapes.

2. **Make the game board.** Glue the gray construction paper to the top of your large box. Place the small box in the center of the lid and trace around its base. Set it aside. Use a ruler and marker to indicate parking spaces on the construction paper. Flatten the box lid and laminate.

Tape the lid tightly to the box bottom. Design a store from the smaller box and glue it to the center of the "parking lot." With the sharp knife, cut 12 slots in the box lid, big enough to hold the wide part of the game pieces. *You may make a more difficult game by increasing the number of pairs and using a larger box.

How to play: Students will take turns pulling two cards from the board. If the bottoms match, the cards are removed. If there is no match, cards are replaced in the original spaces. The student with the most matches at the end of the game is the winner.

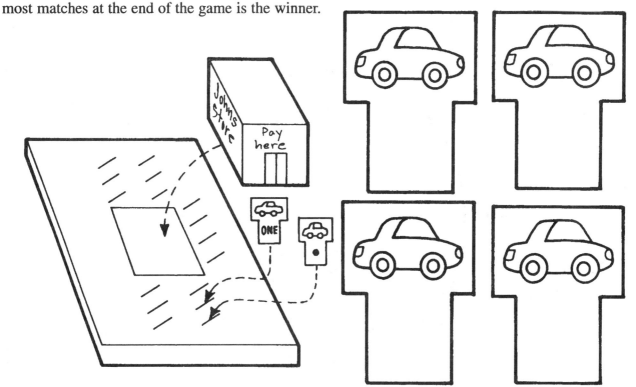

Word Wheel Mobile

What you need:

- one heavy paper plate
- copies of wheel, page 52
- scissors
- yarn six 15-inch (38 cm)
- copies of the patterns (below)
- crayons
- hole punch

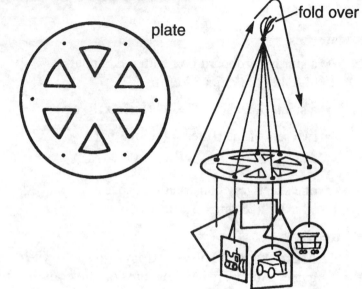

plate

fold over

What you do:

1. Glue the wheel onto a paper plate.
2. Cut away the spaces between the spokes.
3. Color and cut out the six pictures below.
4. Punch holes to tie the yarn at each • on the pictures and on the wheel.
5. To hang, cut and tie six 15-inch (38 cm) yarn lengths through the holes of the plate, as shown.
6. Tie the loose ends of yarn at the top and hang the mobile from the ceiling.

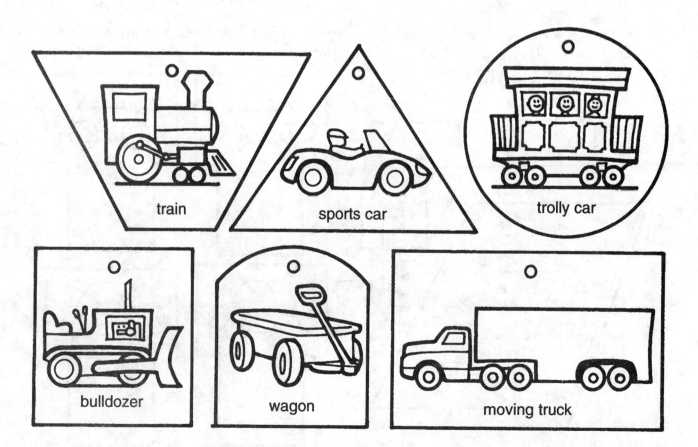

train

sports car

trolly car

bulldozer

wagon

moving truck

Counting Book

1. Count the people on or near the bus.
2. Write the number in the box.
3. Color the pictures. Cut them apart.
4. Staple the pages in order from 1 to 10.

Tire and Wheel Patterns

1. Do you see a pattern? What comes next?

2. Cut out the boxes below.

3. Glue the correct picture in the box.

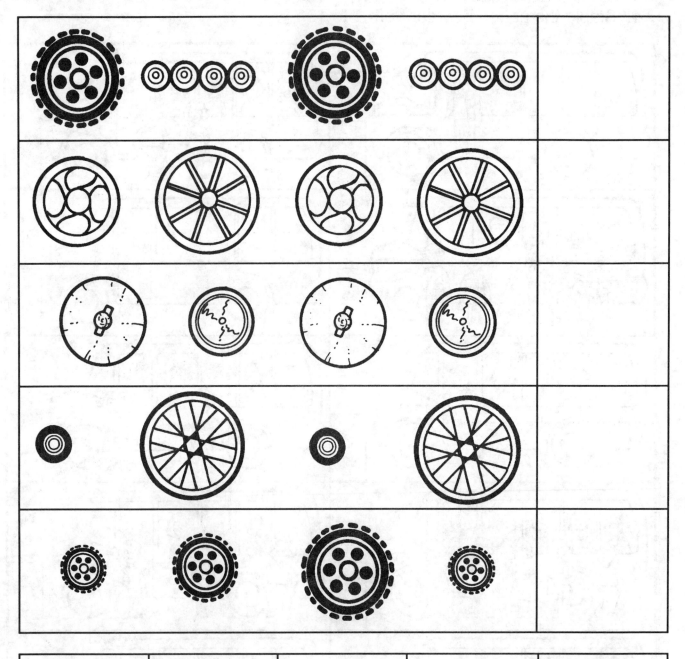

Pickup Truck from Shapes

1. Tell what each shape is.
2. Cut out the shapes.

3. Put the truck together.
4. Glue the truck to another paper.

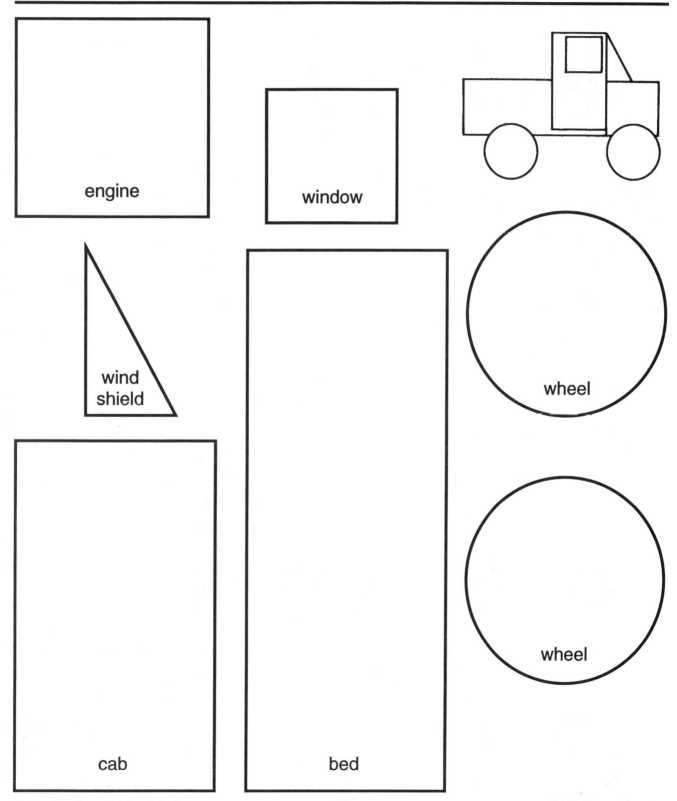

engine

window

wind shield

wheel

wheel

cab

bed

School Bus

1. Draw the driver and some children in the windows.

2. Print your school name on the sides of the bus.

3. Color and cut out the bus.

4. Fold on the dashed lines and glue tabs in place.

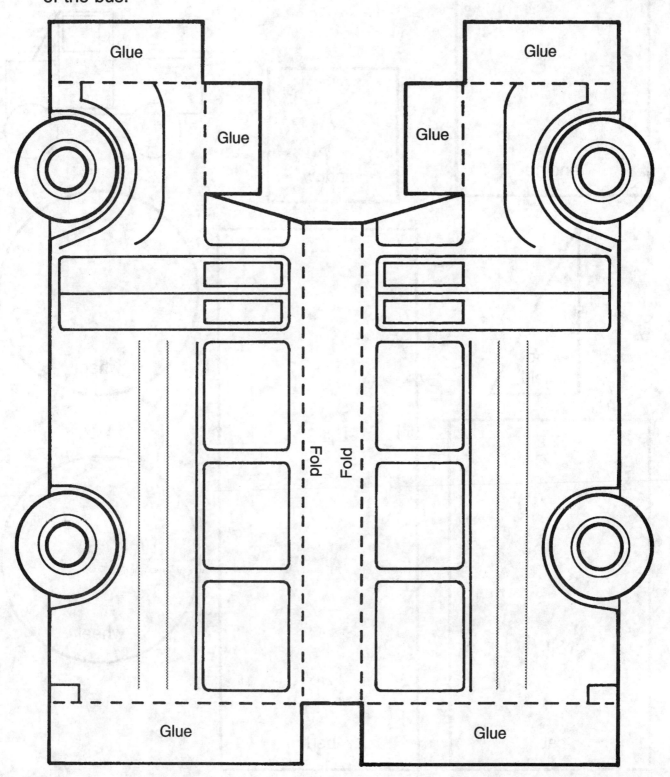

60

Glider

What you need:

- one plastic straw
- two paper clips
- two strips of white paper,
  1" x 9" (3 cm x 23 cm) and
  1" x 6" (3 cm x 15 cm)

What you do:

1. Make loops out of the paper strips and attach them to the ends of the straw with the paper clips. Make sure that both loops are paralle!

2. Hold the glider between your thumb and forefinger with the smallest loop in the front. Push it forward gently so that it will sail. Practice flying the glider through suspended hula hoops or into box targets.

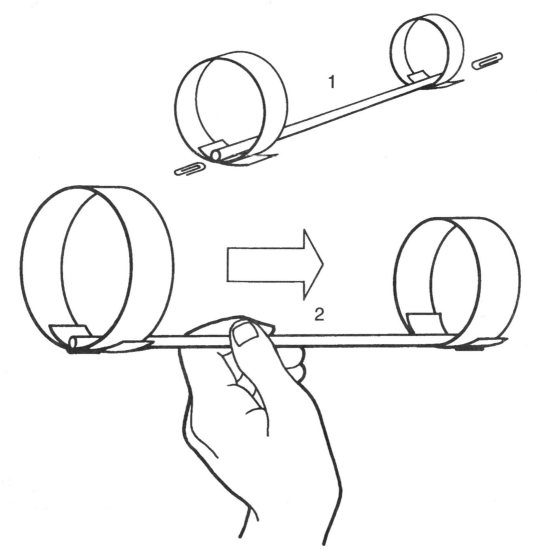

Helicopter

1. Draw a pilot and children in the windows.

2. Color and cut all the pieces.

3. Fold on the dashed lines. Glue **a** on top of **b**.

4. Attach the blades with the paper fasteners.

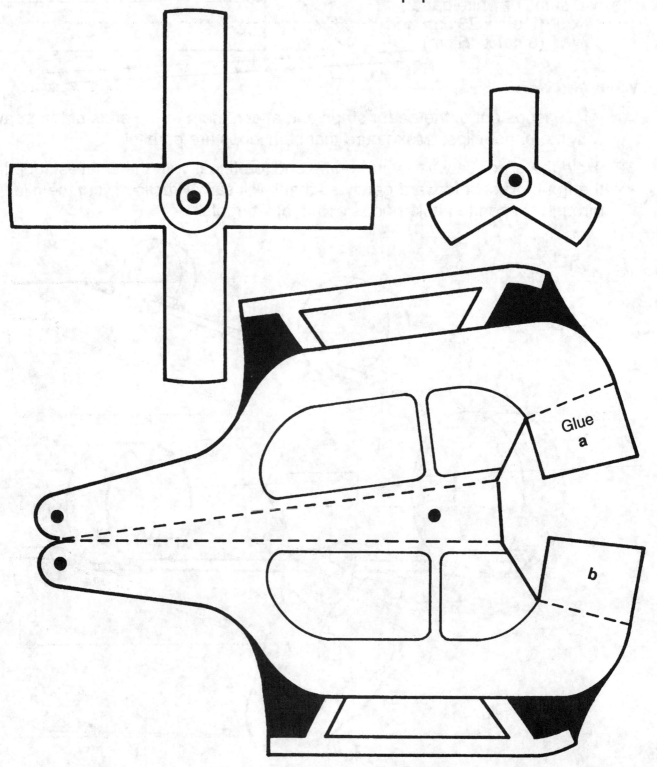

Glue
a

b

62

Fold a Plane

You can make a simple paper airplane that will fly!

1. Fold in number order.
2. Fold on the dashed lines.

3. Do one step at a time.
4. Follow the fold arrows.

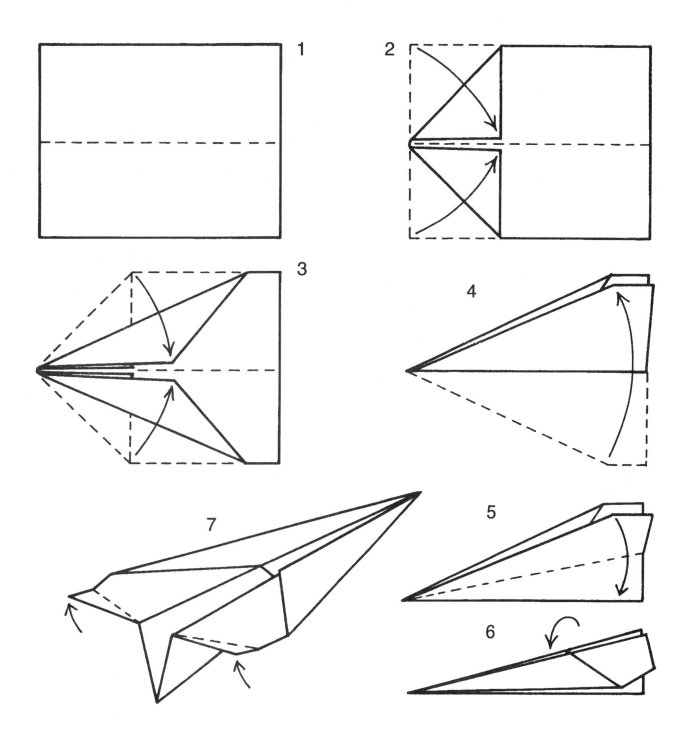

Sailboats

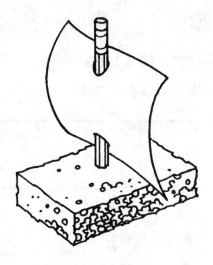

What you need:

- one 2" x 3" (5 cm x 8 cm) pre-cut block of Styrofoam®
- other boat-making materials (sponges, plastic, meat trays, etc.)
- one sharpened pencil (mast) for each boat
- one 2" x 3" (5 cm x 8 cm) paper sail for each boat
- scissors

What you do:

1. Design a sail from the paper. Cut it out.

2. Poke two holes in the paper as shone. Insert the pencil as a mast.

3. Gently twist the pointed end of the pencil into the Styrofoam block.

4. Now make at least two more sailboats out of the other materials.

*Float your sailboats in a tub of water to see which one floats best. Try to explain why or why not.

** Do other experiments with common household items to see which will/will not float. Decide what you think makes some things float. (What are *density, weight*, etc.?) Watch other students with different sizes and types of sponges. Make predictions about whether they will float and which one will sink first.

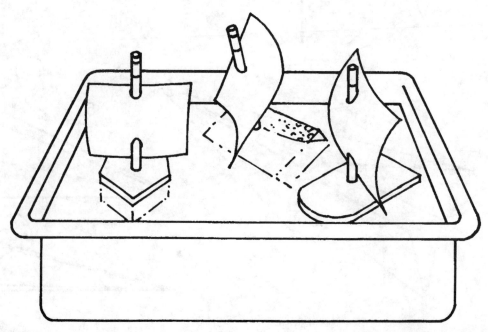

64

Tugboat/Barge

What you need:

- one water table or very large tub to move the barges
- three small foam meat trays
- one foam drinking cup
- one small plastic margarine dish
- twist ties
- hole punch
- stapler
- drinking straw
- small piece of paper (for a flag)
- sand or gravel for *ballast*

What you do: (Experiment)

1. Put some sand or gravel in the margarine dish. Turn the foam cup upside down. Stand it in the margarine dish to create a tugboat wheelhouse.

2. Design a flag. Staple it to the straw. Make a hole and insert the straw into the bottom of the cup.

3. Use the hole punch and twist ties to connect the foam trays to each other and the "tugboat."

4. Put the tugboat and barges in the water. Experiment with putting weight (paper clips, erasers, etc.) on the barges. Record what happens.

What will the barges do?				
Cargo	**Float**		**Sink**	
	1.	2.	1.	2.
Clips				
Erasers				
Crayons				
Gravel				
Wood				
Chips				

Take a class vote:

- How many think it will float?

- How many say sink?

1. Record how many guess for each cargo.

2. Do the experiment. Record your findings.

Wagon/Incline

What you need:

- one small cardboard box
- four cardboard circles for wheels
- two sharpened pencils
- hole punch
- scissors
- stapler

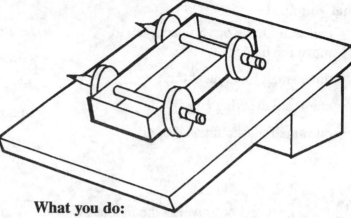

What you do:

1. Cut the four wheels for your wagon.
2. Punch four holes in the sides of your box.
3. Insert the pencils for axles.
4. Attach the wheels to the axles.
5. Check off (✔) each experiment you do below:

_____ Try a variety of toy cars and trucks. Design an incline by leaning a piece of wood against a stack of books. Experiment by running the cars down the ramp. Decide what factors (size, weight) affect the speed of movement.

_____ Try moving the cars sideways down the ramp. What is happing?

_____ Change the degree of the incline higher and lower and make predictions. Record your findings.

_____ Experiment by making wheels of different shapes (square, triangle, octagonal, etc.) Discuss why round wheels are the most efficient.

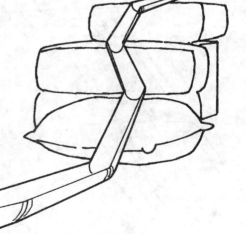

_____ Collect paper towel tubes. Cut them in half lengthwise and tape them together to form a long, twisting, downward track that a toy car can run on without assistance.

66

Safety Signs and Seat Belts

Here are some signs you should know when you are walking.

STOP  Look for traffic before you cross the street.

RAILROAD  Stop, look, and listen for trains before crossing the railroad tracks.

 WALK/DON'T WALK Read these signs before you cross the street.

 CROSSWALK Always cross at the corner and walk inside the crosswalk lines.

Seat Belts

It is important to **always** wear a seat belt when you are riding in a moving air, land, or water vehicle. It will hold you in your seat if there is a sudden stop or an accident? What is wrong with this picture. How can you make it correct?

Be sure to buckle up!

Traffic Light

What you need:

- an empty cardboard tube (from paper towels)
- a copy of the traffic light pattern (page 69)
- crayons or markers

- scissors
- stapler
- glue

What you do:

1. Color one circle on *each side* of the traffic light pattern:

   top, red; — center, yellow; — bottom, green.
2. Cut out the light, fold on the dotted lines, and glue the edges closed.
3. Staple the three-sided traffic light to the top of the cardboard tube.
4. Use your traffic light for playing the game below.

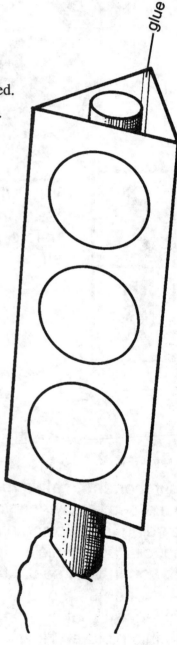

glue tab

Red Light, Green Light, Stop!

Create a road made with masking tape on the floor of your classroom or on the playground. Have your students move like cars and trucks, watching for your signals. They should slow for a yellow light and stop for red. If they do not obey the signals, students will receive "tickets" and have to sit out of the game.

Traffic Light *(cont.)*

(Actual size)

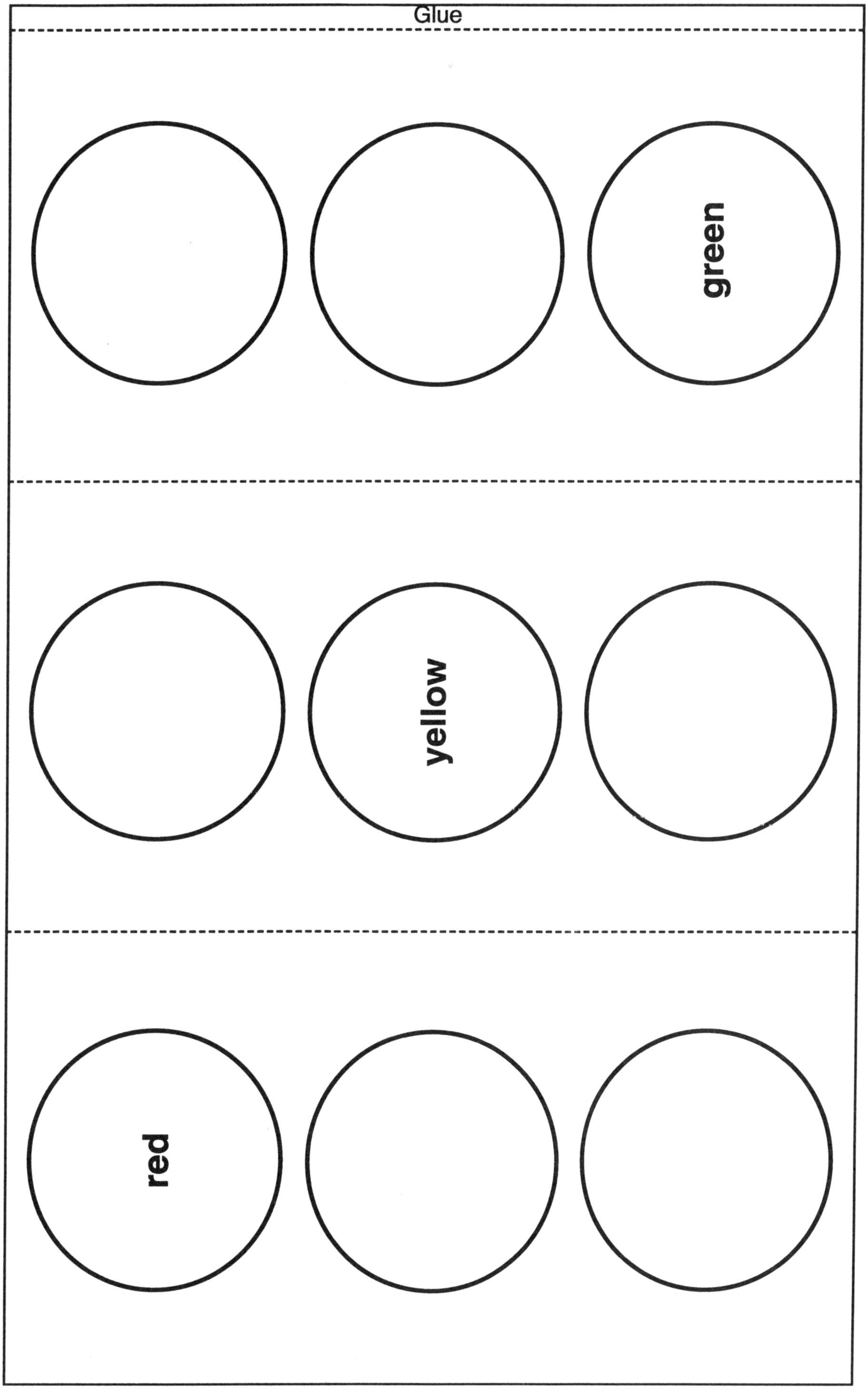

green

yellow

red

Careful Drivers' Day Is Coming

_____

(day, date, and time)

Effective culminations are climactic and memorable!
(Translated: Teachers need a lot of help!)

Adults and students are invited to help us to:

1. **Plan well ahead and prepare with time to spare.** *(Many hands make it light work . . . and great fun!)*

2. **Allow students one week of creative and enjoyable parent/child homework time to make their own cool and crazy cars to drive at our culmination day.**

3. **Recruit parents and/or a few older students to help prepare the following:**

   - a traffic light (pattern on pages 68 and 69),

   - an assortment of handheld signs: *Caution, Stop, Walk, Don't Walk . . .*

   - a few special signs: *Railroad Crossing, Pedestrian Crossing, School Bus Stop and Crossing, Hospital–Quiet Please, Skunk Crossing* (with a picture). We are counting on you to think of more!

4. **Join other volunteers that morning to head outdoors, with wide masking tape and our detailed neighborhood map, to lay out some intersections and crosswalks.** Depending on space and help, "mappers" (using simple paper signs) might also designate the following:

   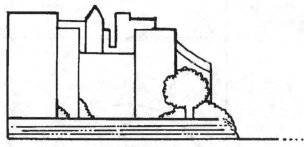

   - local street names
   - students' homes
   - recreation areas
   - special buildings (school, store, hospital, police station, fire station, traffic school, car wash, Travelers' Aid Station, Traffic Officers' Posts).

   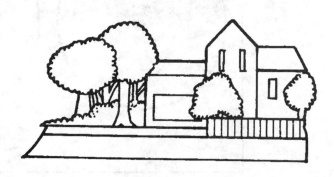

   - directional signs (*North Pole, South Pole, East Coast, West Coast*) and *GO!* (spot where the drivers start)
   - any other signs you can come up with to make it more interesting and educational. (What a way to take a test!)

Careful Drivers' Day Is Coming *(cont.)*

5. **Direct the students who are taking turns operating the signals while others drive or walk.**

6. **Just for fun, be the adult traffic officer or student safety patrol** (maybe wear a dark uniform, badge and belt if you're really into this) **and give out the following:**

   - citations (designed with the chief's stamp of approval to make them official)
   - positive buttons   (Wow! I'm a Junior Safety Patrol Officer.)
   - traffic citations *(Cited for ___Safe Driving___. Drive directly to traffic school. Do not pass GO!)*
   - award certificates for Outstanding Driving Skills and Good Citizen Driver

7. **Volunteer for an hour shift:**

   - Travelers' Aid Station—serve lemonade and other refreshments graciously supplied by none other than . . . our students and parents (from the easy and delicious recipes on pages 74 and 75. YUMMY! YUMMY!).
   - Traffic Officers Posts—direct traffic and assist tourists in finding local hot spots (using a great deal of north, south, east, west and left, right, of course)
   - ??? With your wonderfully creative minds helping, we'll think of more by the big day!

8. **Create cards with directions for errands and emergencies.**

   - *Baby's crying. Mom is out of milk! Where do I go for help?*
   - *A skunk caught Dad. Take him to the car wash!*
   -
   -
   -
   -
   -
   -
   -
   -
   -
   -
   -

   Add your own suggestions.

   _____
   (Teacher's signature)

Culminating Activity

Cool and Crazy Cars

Coming your way on _____ !

day, date, time

We'll be testing our understanding of traffic signs and signals while we drive our own life-sized cars. Parents are encouraged to help their child build a car as homework and bring it on the big day. We'll please practice driving slowly and safely at home and share what we've learned about traffic signs and signals, directions, and the rules of the road, before driving at school for our driver's test. We appreciate your help in building a cool and crazy car.

What you need:
- One large cardboard box
- Four large heavy paper plate wheels
- Two small paper plate headlights
- One tagboard for 6" x 9" license plate (15 cm x 23 cm)
- One 12" (30 cm) clear laminated plastic for windshield
- Masking tape to attach windshield
- Four $1\frac{3}{4}$" (5 cm) paper fasteners (to attach wheels)
- Several colors of tempera paint/brushes
- Scissors and glue
- Wide heavy cloth tape

What you do: (after you've studied the above sketch):

1. Cut a large "body" hole out of the bottom of the box.

2. Cut another "body" hole from the top. Leave a square piece attached at the front to fold up for the windshield. Cut out the center of the windshield, leaving only a wide windshield frame for the plastic.

3. Add any creative touches to complete your own design.

4. Paint it. **Important: Allow it all to dry at least one day.**

5. Attach headlights and wheels etc.

6. Design a license plate. Glue it onto the front. Add a name plate on the back.

7. Glue or tape the laminated plastic inside the windshield section. Trim along the outside frame.

8. To attach the heavy tape shoulder straps, experiment to see what is most comfortable before poking holes in the sides of the car. You might wear the straps front to back, over your shoulders, with tiny belt loops to hold them in place, or diagonally from left front corner to right back corner, and perhaps another from right front over to left back, if needed. What works for one student may not work for another. **Take care not to wrap anything <u>around </u>the neck, even if it feels comfortable.** Don't forget your seat belt!

Street Playmat

Note to teacher: This project may be as elaborate as time and supplies permit. If it is made well, it can provide hours of creative play long after the transportation unit is completed. Explain that you will be designing a simple map of an imaginary town. Ask your students what they would like to include: streets, a lake or harbor, an airport, stores (with parking lots), houses, school, and a playground, etc. Children will bring their own toy cars, boats, trains, and planes from home. They will use the playmat, in appropriate play, to simulate daily life in a busy city, to tell stories, and to respond to teacher directions.

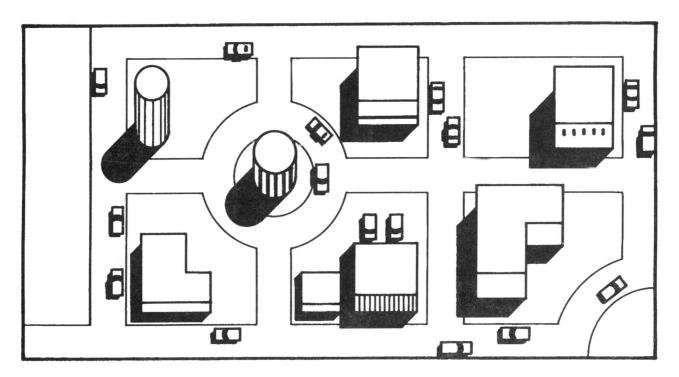

What you need for the playmat:
- white shower curtain liner
- permanent marker(s)
- black plastic tape (optional)

What you need for the buildings:
- small boxes
- construction paper
- art supplies

What you do:
1. With pencil, draw the roads on the white plastic until they are in the proper positions.
2. Trace pencil lines with markers or cover the road lines with black plastic tape.
3. Encourage each child to bring a small box to create a building (small milk cartons are great for houses). Ask for student suggestions and assign a variety of buildings. Encourage them to use lots of color and detail in their creations.
4. When they finish, spread out your playmat and set the buildings in place.
5. For ongoing learning opportunities, ask students and parents to look at their real world and suggest activities for the playmat. You may be pleasantly surprised at what they suggest.

Recipes

Pinwheels (4 servings)

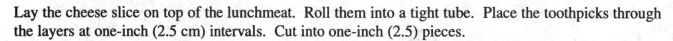

- 1 slice of lunchmeat (cut square to fit the cheese)
- 1 slice of yellow cheese
- toothpicks
- knife   (**Note:** used only by an adult)
- waxed paper (to cover the table)

Lay the cheese slice on top of the lunchmeat. Roll them into a tight tube. Place the toothpicks through the layers at one-inch (2.5 cm) intervals. Cut into one-inch (2.5) pieces.

Tuna Boats (4 servings)

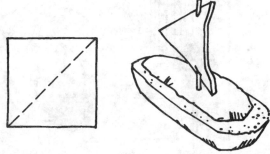
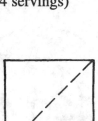

- one hot dog roll
- one cup of tuna salad
- two slices of cheese (any kind)
- serving spoon
- knife (**Note:** used only by an adult)
- four plastic coffee stirrers
- waxed paper (to cover the table)

Cut the hot dog roll into halves. Remove some of the bread from the center. Fill with ¼ (63 mL) cup of tuna salad. Cut the cheese slices in half diagonally for sails. Make two holes in each sail and carefully insert the coffee stirrer like a mast. Stand the sail upright in the tuna salad.

Hot Dog Hot Rod (1 serving)

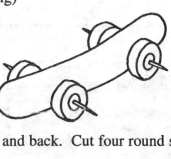

- one hot dog
- two toothpicks
- one carrot
- knife (**Note:** used only by an adult)
- waxed paper (to cover the table)

Insert the toothpicks all the way through the hot dog in the front and back. Cut four round slices from the carrot. Insert the carrots onto the toothpicks like wheels.

Airplane Cake (serves the entire class)

- one 9" x 13" (23 cm x 33.5 cm) prepared sheet cake
- one can of prepared icing
- cake decorations (optional)
- knife   (**Note:** used only by an adult)

Cut the cake as shown. Assemble the pieces on a large platter. Ice and decorate the cake as an airplane.

74

Recipes *(cont.)*

Skateboards (2 servings)

- four oval or rectangular crackers
- ¼ cup (63 mL) smooth peanut butter (or jelly)
- 4 pretzel sticks
- a package of fruit flavored roll candy
- knife (**Note:** used only by an adult)
- waxed paper (to cover the table)

Spread peanut butter or jelly on one cracker. Lay two pretzel sticks across the filling as shown (to be the axles). Put the other cracker on top. Insert the roll candy onto the pretzel sticks for wheels.

*If you prefer, make a wagon from the same ingredients. Use the pretzel stick as a handle and "glue" the roll candy wheels in place with a dab of peanut butter. **Note:** People can be highly allergic to peanut butter. Check with parents regarding food allergies.

Wagon Wheel Cookies

- one or two packages of round, sturdy cookies (oatmeal)–2 per student
- one can of icing
- one package of licorice whips
- knife (**Note:** used only by an adult)
- clean scissors
- waxed paper (to cover the table)

Ice the cookies. Cut the licorice into pieces with scissors and press it in place like the spokes of a wheel.

Celery Sailboat
(Serves the entire class)

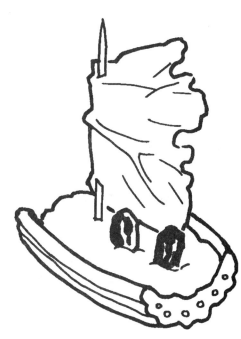

- one bunch of celery
- peanut butter, cream cheese, or other cheese spread
- one bunch of leaf lettuce
- raisins
- toothpicks
- knife (**Note:** used only by an adult)
- waxed paper (to cover the table)

Wash the celery. Cut into three-inch (8 cm) lengths. Fill with peanut butter or cheese. Wash and dry the leaf lettuce. Tear it into two-inch (5 cm) pieces. Insert a toothpick into the rib of the lettuce and stand it in the celery like a sail. Insert several raisin "sailors" in the boat.

Bulletin Board

These interactive bulletin boards are decorations as well as learning activities. They are best adapted for a relatively small area and used with a group of four children.

What you need:

- white background paper
- copies of the Vocabulary Words and Pictures (pages 7 and 8)
- magazine pictures of people, mounted on tagboard

- scissors, glue
- crayons, paint
- pushpins or thumb tacks

What you do:

1. Cover the entire bulletin board with white paper.

2. Color or paint a simple background showing land, sea, and sky.

3. Add a road with traffic signs and a railroad track with a crossing.

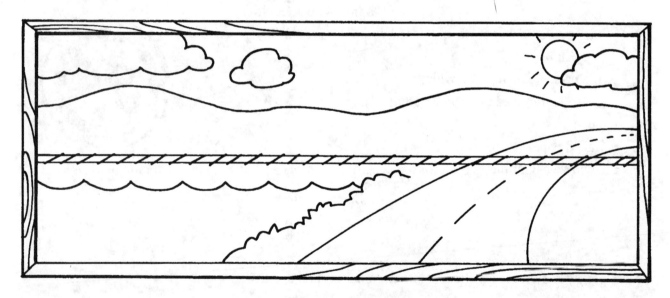

Suggested Uses

1. Arrange the picture cards of people and vehicles into an interesting scene. Tell a story, expressing the action or describing the scene. Use color and number words whenever possible. Print the story on chart paper. Practice reading the story together.

2. Have one group of students put the vehicle pictures in place on the board. A second group will attach the correct word label.

3. Place the vehicles incorrectly on the board (airplane in the water, etc.). Have your students rearrange them correctly.

4. Have students show understanding of antonyms (opposites) by moving the vehicles in response to word cards. (Antonyms: up/down, high/low, fast/slow, front/back, stop/go, top/bottom, left/right.)

Learning Centers

Learning Centers are best when they are small and simple. They provide students opportunities for independent learning—at their own pace and in their best modality. Centers will broaden and enliven your students knowledge, most noticeably in language skills, brainstorming, and sharing with a small group what they already know. Centers build responsibility, good study skills, and self-esteem. Start out slowly with just one center at a time, always teaching how to use the materials and how to clean up properly. Then insist on appropriate behavior. Adapt centers to your students and your classroom situation. (Try ceiling center signs and a plant or two.)

A Story Time Center invites students to come often and sit comfortably as they hear and informally discuss stories being read aloud to them. Your nearest carpet dealer usually has remnants or outdated carpet samples. A few pillows will have students eagerly sneaking off to a "Good Worker Reward," quietly sharing a story with a friend or a snuggly stuffed mascot.

A Book Center is also for displaying any object that goes with your books. Ask for book donations from older students. Ask a parent volunteer to take the bibliography on page 80 to the nearest library, check out the limit, but do not allow class and library books to mix.

A Listening Center can be nearby on the floor, just a pillow, a small tape recorder, headphone, and a basket for storing the tapes, will allow students to listen and sing all the poems, stories, and songs *that you recorded when you presented them in class*. Tape record sharing time! It is a great spot to hear again, close up, all about those visuals and independent projects from home(unbreakable please.) Insist that they must relate to the unit being studied and they should be very sturdy.

An Art Center can be a low table covered with butcher paper for easy cleaning. Three small baby food paint jars (allowing for experimenting with the basic color combinations) can be discarded frequently. A plastic diaper pail will keep clay moist for "travel" creativity, along with a low shelf for drying and painting. The possibilities are endless, and the choices are child's play.

A Craft Center nearby provides boxes full of various sizes and shapes of discarded wood, wheels, and dowel pieces. Often parents will volunteer to check the discard pile at their local lumber store and keep you well-supplied. Display pictures of cars, trains, trucks, boats, etc., to inspire creativity (and a small bottle of wood glue.) A small shelf will encourage displaying (and stories). These can be painted at the art center.

A Writing Center can be an extra desk containing paper and pencil. Enclose with a cardboard box "study carrel" to display *Works in Progress* and *Finished Products*. Post related pictures and captions to stimulate imagination and give subtle direction. It quickly becomes a favorite center!

A Role-Play Center allows for dressing up and pretending to be drivers, pilots, boat captains, etc. Provide a variety of shirts and hats (and a place to hang them) and assorted travel toys for acting out at story time and independent playtime. Often older students are willing to donate outgrown costumes, hats, and toys. Advertise for what you need in local schools and churches.

An Activity Center has the greatest flexibility of all. Simple shelves are all that are needed. This is where the manipulatives, learning games, and puzzles are stored and enjoyed. Many of the travel-related activities described in this book are suitable for independent projects here. A bulletin board above can display the finished products. A table is nice, but children love the floor.

Songs and Games

Several traditional songs are appropriate for this unit. The following is a sampling of songs and games that young children have enjoyed through the years. Encourage children to invent their own verses, using easy rhyming words for "New River Train," *The Raffi Singable Songbook*, Crown, 1987, or act out the words of the favorite, "Wheels on the Bus," *The 2nd Raffi Songbook,* Crown, 1986. "I've Been Working on the Railroad" can be found on *More Singable Songs* by (MCA Recording, Troubador Records, Ltd., 1997).

Be sure to check the simple folk song "Train Is a Comin'," *The Fun to Sing Songbook* by Esther L. Nelson, Sterling Publishers, 1986. It is very repetitious but has several verses with the possibility of creating many more. Other traditional songs include "Row, Row, Row Your Boat," "Down By the Station," and "Lightly Row," all found in *Singing Bee!* compiled by Jane Hart, Lothrop, Lee and Shepard, 1982. Also in that book are "The Gallant Ship" (an English Traditional Singing Game) and "See the Pony Galloping, Galloping" (an American folk song) which suggest large muscle movements.

New River Train

I'm riding on that new river train,

Riding on that new river train,

Same old train that brought me here,

Gonna carry me back again.

Darlin' you can't love one . . .

Darlin' you can't love one . . .

You can't love one and still have fun, oh,

Darlin' you can't love one.

Darlin' you can't love two . . .

(repeat)

You can't love two and still be true, oh,

Darlin' you can't love two.

Darlin' you can't love three . . .

(repeat)

You can't love three and still have me, oh,

Darlin' you can't love three . . .

(repeat)

*Continue this pattern for verses four to ten.

Wheels on the Bus

The wheels on the bus go round and round,

Round and round, round and round,

The wheels on the bus go round and round,

All through the town.

The wipers on the bus

Go swish, swish, swish . . .

The people on the bus

Go up and down . . .

The driver on the bus

Says "Move on back!" . . .

The horn on the bus

Goes beep, beep, beep . . .

This award is given to

_____

for successfully completing the unit on

Things That Go!

_____   _____

Teacher   Date

This award is given to

_____

for successfully completing the unit on

Things That Go!

_____   _____

Teacher   Date

Bibliography

Air

Anderson, Joan. *Harry's Helicopter.* Morrow Junior Books, 1990.

Barton, Byron. *Airplanes.* Crowell, 1986.

Browne, Gerald. *The Aircraft Lift-the-Flap Book.* Dutton, 1991.

Crews, Donald. *Flying.* Greenwillow Books, 1986.

McPhail, David. *First Flight.* Little, Brown, 1987.

Royston, Angela. *My Lift-the-Flap Plane Book.* G.P. Putnam, 1993.

Siebert, Diane. *Plane Song.* Harper Collins, 1993.

Land

Borden, Louise. *The Neighborhood Trucker.* Scholastic, 1990.

Conoway, Judith. *Things That Go!* Troll, 1987.

Crews, Donald. *Bicycle Race.* Greenwillow Books, 1985.

Crews, Donald. *Freight Train.* Greenwillow Books, 1978.

Crews, Donald. *School Bus.* Greenwillow Books, 1984.

Crews, Donald. *Shortcut.* Greenwillow Books, 1992.

Crews, Donald. *Truck.* Greenwillow Books, 1980.

Dodds, Dayle Ann. *Wheel Away.* Harper Trophy, 1989.

Jonas, Ann. *Round Trip.* Greenwillow Books, 1983.

McHenry, Ellen Johnston. *Inside a Freight Train.* Cobblehill, 1993.

Morris, Ann. *On the Go.* Lothrop, Lee and Shepard, 1990.

Mott, Evelyn Clark. *Steam Train Ride.* Walker, 1991.

Pomerantz, Charlotte. *How Many Trucks Can a Tow Truck Tow?* Random House, 1987.

Royston, Angela. *Cars.* Aladdin, 1991.

Scarry, Richard. *Cars and Trucks and Things That Go.* Western, 1974.

Schreier, Joshua. *Luigi's All-Night Parking Lot.* Dutton, 1990.

Siebert, Diane. *Train Song.* Crowell, 1981.

Stine, Megan. *Wheels! The Kids' Bicycle Book.* Little, Brown, 1990.

Wilson, Sarah. *Garage Song.* Simon and Schuster, 1991.

Zelinsky, Paul. *The Wheels on the Bus.* Dutton, 1990.

Sea

Crews, Donald. *Harbor.* Greenwillow, 1982.

Gibbons, Gail. *Boat Book.* Holiday House, 1983.

Gramatky, Hardie. *Little Toot.* G. P. Putnam, 1967.

Henderson, Kathy. *The Little Boat.* Candelwick, 1995.

Maestro, Betsy. *Big City Port.* Four Winds, 1983.

McDonnell, Flora. *I Love Boats.* Candelwick, 1995.

Robbins, Ken. *Boats.* Scholastic, 1989.

Technology

Alphabet Express. disk, Apple, IBM, Software Shop.

Field Trip to the Airport. CD, Mac, Win, Educational Resources.

How Things Work in Busy Town. CD-ROM, Windows or Mac, Win, Paramount Interactive.

Let's Explore the Airport with Buzzy. CD, WIN CD, Educational Resources.

Putt-Putt Joins the Parade. CD-ROM, MPC, National School Products.

Race Car 'Rithmetic. 256K, CGA, National School Products.

Ships Ahoy Math Builder. 256K, CGA, National School Products.

Space Shuttle. disk, 640K, VGA, National School Products.

Stickybear Town Builder. 640K, CGA, National School Products.

Talking School Bus. disk, 512K, CGA, National School Products.